PEOPLE OF THE COVENANT

God's New Covenant for Today

Jack W. Hayford
with
Paul McGuire

THOMAS NELSON PUBLISHERS
Nashville

CONTENTS

People of the Covenant: God's New Covenant for Today is one of a series of study guides that focus exciting, discovery-geared coverage of Bible book and power themes—all prompting toward dynamic, Holy Spirit-filled living.

About the Executive Editor

JACK W. HAYFORD, noted pastor, teacher, writer, and composer, is the Executive Editor of the complete series, working with the publisher in the conceiving and developing of each of the books.

Dr. Hayford is Senior Pastor of The Church On The Way, the First Foursquare Church of Van Nuys, California. He and his wife, Anna, have four married children, all of whom are active in either pastoral ministry or vital church life. As General Editor of the *Spirit-Filled Life Bible,* Pastor Hayford led a four-year project, which has resulted in the availability of one of today's most practical and popular study Bibles. He is author of more than twenty books, including *A Passion for Fullness, The Beauty of Spiritual Language, Rebuilding the Real You,* and *Prayer Is Invading the Impossible.* His musical compositions number over four hundred songs, including the widely sung "Majesty."

About the Writer

PAUL McGUIRE is an author of increasing breadth of acceptance and demand, his ministry becoming noted for his spiritual sensitivity and forthrightness in addressing the New Age philosophy with practical and biblical wisdom. His local church and conference ministry effectively deals with pathways to restoring marriage, being healed from a broken past, and learning to minister to people in the New Age environment. His gift on these themes is enhanced by the way Paul confronts without condemning.

He was a student in psychology at the University of Missouri, and now lives in Santa Clarita, California, with his wife, Kristina, and their three children: Paul (age 3) and twins Michael and Jennifer (age 1). The family is an active part of the congregation served by Dr. Hayford.

Paul McGuire's books include *Evangelizing the New Age, Supernatural Faith in the New Age, Marriage Breakthrough,* and *Healing from the Past.* Of this contributor, the Executive Editor has remarked: "Paul is becoming a Holy Spirit instrument of pure and tender power in assisting victims of contemporary marital confusion and popularized error to come into spiritual liberty through Jesus Christ."

THE KEYS
THAT KEEP ON FREEING

Is there anything that holds more mystery or more genuine practicality than a key? The mystery: "What does it fit? What can it turn on? What might it open? What new discovery could be made? The practicality: Something *will* most certainly open to the possessor! Something *will* absolutely be found to unlock and allow a possibility otherwise obstructed!

- Keys describe the instruments we use to access or ignite.
- Keys describe the concepts that unleash mind-boggling possibilities.
- Keys describe the different structures of musical notes which allow variation and range.

Jesus spoke of keys: "And I will give you the keys of the kingdom of heaven, and whatever you bind on earth will be bound in heaven, and whatever you loose on earth will be loosed in heaven" (Matt. 16:19).

While there is no conclusive list of exactly what keys Jesus was referring to, it is clear that He did confer upon His church—upon *all* who believe—the access to a realm of spiritual partnership with Him in the dominion of His kingdom. Faithful students of the Word of God, moving in the practical grace and biblical wisdom of Holy Spirit-filled living and ministry, have noted some of the primary themes which undergird this order of "spiritual partnership" Christ offers. The "keys" are *concepts*—biblical themes that are traceable through the Scriptures and verifiably dynamic when applied with soundly based faith under the lordship of Jesus Christ. The "partnership" is the *essential* feature of this release of divine grace;

(1) believers reaching to *receive* Christ's promise of "kingdom keys," (2) while choosing to *believe* in the Holy Spirit's readiness to actuate their unleashing, unlimited power today.

Companioned with the Bible book studies in the *Spirit-Filled Life Study Guide* series, the Kingdom Dynamic studies present a dozen different themes. This study series is an outgrowth of the Kingdom Dynamics themes included throughout the *Spirit-Filled Life Bible*, which provide a treasury of insight developed by some of today's most respected Christian leaders. From that beginning, studious writers have evolved the elaborated studies you'll pursue here.

The central goal of the subjects focused on in this present series of study guides is to relate "power points" of the Holy Spirit-filled life. Assisting you in your discoveries are a number of helpful features. Each study guide has twelve to fourteen lessons, each arranged so you can plumb the depths or skim the surface, depending upon your needs and interests. The study guides contain major lesson features, each marked by a symbol and heading for easy identification.

WORD WEALTH

The WORD WEALTH feature provides important definitions of key terms.

BEHIND THE SCENES

BEHIND THE SCENES supplies information about cultural beliefs and practices, doctrinal disputes, business trades, and the like, that illuminate Bible passages and teachings.

AT A GLANCE

The AT A GLANCE feature uses maps and charts to identify places and simplify themes or positions.

 KINGDOM EXTRA

Because this study guide focuses on a theme of the Bible, you will find a KINGDOM EXTRA feature that guides you into Bible dictionaries, Bible encyclopedias, and other resources that will enable you to glean more from the Bible's wealth on the topic if you want something extra.

 PROBING THE DEPTHS

Another feature, PROBING THE DEPTHS, will explain controversial issues raised by particular lessons and cite Bible passages and other sources to which you can turn to help you come to your own conclusions.

 FAITH ALIVE

Finally, each lesson contains a FAITH ALIVE feature. Here the focus is, So what? Given what the Bible says, what does it mean for my life? How can it impact my day-to-day needs, hurts, relationships, concerns, and whatever else is important to me? FAITH ALIVE will help you see and apply the practical relevance of God's literary gift.

As you'll see, these guides supply space for you to answer the study and life-application questions and exercises. You may, however, want to record all your answers, or just the overflow from your study or application, in a separate notebook or journal. This would be especially helpful if you think you'll dig into the KINGDOM EXTRA features. Because the exercises in this feature are optional and can be expanded as far as you want to take them, we have not allowed writing space for them in this study guide. So you may want to have a notebook or journal handy for recording your discoveries while working through to this feature's riches.

The Bible study method used in this series revolves around four basic steps: observation, interpretation, correlation, and application. Observation answers the question, What does the text say? Interpretation deals with, What does the text mean? —not with what it means to you or me, but what it meant to its original readers. Correlation asks, What light do other Scripture passages shed on this text? And application, the goal of Bible study, poses the question, How should my life change in response to the Holy Spirit's teaching of this text?

If you have used a Bible much before, you know that it comes in a variety of translations and paraphrases. Although you can use any of them with profit as you work through the *Spirit-Filled Life Kingdom Dynamics Study Guide* series, when Bible passages or words are cited, you will find they are from the New King James Version of the Bible. Using this translation with this series will make your study easier, but it's certainly not necessary.

The only resources you need to complete and apply these study guides are a heart and mind open to the Holy Spirit, a prayerful attitude, and a pencil and a Bible. Of course, you may draw upon other sources, such as commentaries, dictionaries, encyclopedias, atlases, and concordances, and you'll even find some optional exercises that will guide you into these sources. But these are extras, not necessities. These study guides are comprehensive enough to give you all you need to gain a good, basic understanding of the Bible book being covered and how you can apply its themes and counsel to your life.

A word of warning, though. By itself, Bible study will not transform your life. It will not give you power, peace, joy, comfort, hope, and a number of other gifts God longs for you to unwrap and enjoy. Through Bible study, you will grow in your understanding of the Lord, His kingdom and your place in it, and those things are essential. But you need more. You need to rely on the Holy Spirit to guide your study and your application of the Bible's truths. He, Jesus promised, was sent to teach us "all things" (John 14:26; cf. 1 Cor. 2:13). So as you use this series to guide you through Scripture, bathe your study time in prayer, asking the Spirit of God to illuminate the text, enlighten your mind, humble your will, and comfort your heart. He will never let you down.

My prayer and goal for you is that as you unlock and begin to explore God's Book for living His way, the Holy Spirit will fill every fiber of your being with the joy and power God longs to give all His children. So read on. Be diligent. Stay open and submissive to Him. You will not be disappointed. He promises you!

Introduction

All of us who have believed the gospel of Jesus Christ find ourselves on a path, growing in faith and love. Like Mary, we ponder things in our hearts. We wonder about this and that until the Holy Spirit shows us. And then we are filled with wonder and worship at the grandeur of His plan.

Let this study guide be a tool in your hand to discover more of God's rich inheritance to you in Christ.

As a former New Age seeker, I read widely in philosophy and other academic disciplines. What a contrast there is between such learning and the discovery of reality—THE reality of God's love in Jesus, the real, resurrected Person, made approachable through His blood and through His Word—the Bible.

In this study I have included some rival philosophies and religious viewpoints to help you appreciate how far God's thoughts exceed even the very best ideas the world can offer. Remember, Christianity is not a religion; it is *truth*. In fact, it is THE Truth.

The *Blood* and the *Bible*. The blood of Jesus Christ and the Word of the living God. You may wonder: "What practical application does the blood of Jesus have in my everyday living? I understand the importance of daily Bible reading and applying its truths to my life, but the blood? I know the blood of Jesus is important, but how?"

As you study, you will learn that we are people of the Covenant—a Covenant characterized by *both* blood and a book. You will find that these are far more than symbols. Both are cleansing agents. Both are weapons to be wielded in our spiritual conflict with darkness. Both are connected in at least three other ways:

1. The *scrolls* and the mercy seat were sprinkled with *blood* (Heb. 9:19, 21).

2. *Blood* flowed from *Jesus'* side. Jesus is God's Word made flesh (John 1:14; 19:34).

3. Our Lord's communion table is prepared with both *wine* and *bread* (Matt. 4:4; 26:26–28; John 6:32–58; 1 Cor. 11:24, 25).

As you move down the path of wondering to the wonder of His plan, let these stepping stones help chart your way:

PEOPLE OF THE COVENANT:
GOD'S NEW COVENANT FOR TODAY

1 The Blood of the Covenant

2 The Authority of God's Word

3 The Blood of the Covering | Disobedience to the Word

4 Abel's Sacrifice | Obedience to the Word

5 The Blood of Jesus

6 The Power of God's Word

7 The Lamb Who Takes Away Sin

8 Access to God Through the Blood

9 Fruit of the Word

10 Communion

11 The Promises of God's Word

12 The Blood of the Lamb | The Word of Their Testimony

13 Conclusion

As you study the thirteen lessons in this book, you'll discover:

Concerning the BLOOD

God is a God who makes covenants—blood-sealed covenants—for the purpose of establishing a right relationship with us, His children. God, who is perfect and true, has revealed Himself in His Word, the Bible, which is perfect and true (ch. 1).

Jesus Himself is the ultimate, once-for-all, blood Sacrifice who has opened the way boldly to approach Father God and confidently live in the power of the Holy Spirit (ch. 5).

The blood of Jesus the Lamb of God is also powerful. It protects, purges, and pulverizes Satan our enemy (ch. 7).

It cleanses us, giving us a clear conscience and a love for others (ch. 8).

Concerning the WORD

The Bible not only measures our lives and our words, but it also shows us how to live and speak (ch. 2).

The Author of the Bible makes His Word both powerful and practical. He makes it apply to all the "nitty-gritty" living of His readers and hearers (ch. 6).

The Word of God is like food to be eaten or seed to be sown, bringing growth and yielding harvest (ch. 9).

God's promises are "exceedingly great and precious." We begin to see how this is true (ch. 11).

Concerning both the BLOOD and the WORD

To obey or disobey? That is the question with God's Word. Our disobedience created a need not only for our tracks to be covered, but for us to be covered (ch. 3).

Abel believed God's Word and obediently brought a blood offering to the Lord (ch. 4).

Communion is more than a sacrament (ch. 10).

Revelation 12:11 says that believers overcome their adversary "by the blood of the Lamb and by the word of their testimony" (ch. 12).

History's final chapter has the Lamb of God "in the midst of [heaven's] throne" (Rev. 5:6) and His Word is forever (Matt. 24:35). Living with Christ's return in view brings great hope and purpose to the present (ch. 13).

Note: The verse(s) in parentheses, following most questions in this study guide, suggest a possible starting point in your search of the Scriptures to help you write your response. Sometimes the parenthetical verse will be from the Scripture portion currently in focus at that point in the chapter. At other times, it will be an additional verse to refer to.

Lesson 1/Understanding the Blood of the Covenant

It is important that, as believers in Jesus Christ, we fully understand what the Bible teaches about the blood of the covenant. We live in an age of cultural relativism. The truth that God has structured the universe in such a way that we can only come to Him through the blood of Jesus Christ is difficult to understand. In fact, to many in our society who believe that they are enlightened or even on a higher plane of consciousness, Christianity is viewed as some kind of primitive blood-stained religion. The question is constantly raised, "Why can't I come to God my own way? Why do I need to accept Jesus Christ?" The truth—that it is only through the death and resurrection of Christ and through the shedding of His blood that we can be cleansed of our sins—is not only misunderstood, but challenged.

In understanding the blood of the covenant, the key question must be asked: Why is it only through the blood that my sins can be forgiven?

GOD AS THE COVENANT-MAKER
(Genesis 1:3–5; 8:20)

Pick up a Bible, and begin to read it and flip through its pages. It is amazing to see the continuity of thought from Genesis to Revelation. It is like one enormous tapestry woven by a Master Artist whose thousands of threads come together in an incredibly intricate design of color and patterns. The Bible has specific themes that are developed and carried through perfectly by different men and women over centuries of time. One such key theme in Scripture is the concept that God is a "covenant-maker."

Beginning in Genesis 1:3–5, we are introduced to God as the God of the covenant:

> Then God said, "Let there be light"; and there was light. And God saw the light, that *it* was good; and God divided the light from the darkness. God called the light Day, and the darkness He called Night. So the evening and the morning were the first day.

At the very beginning of Creation, God reveals Himself as the Covenant-Maker. Jeremiah gives us further understanding of this idea of God's activity in Creation as acts of covenant.

According to Jeremiah what is as unbreakable as God's covenant with creation? (33:20, 21)

COVENANT OF DAY + NIGHT

IF YOU CAN BREAK THE COVENANT WITH THE DAY + NIGHT SO THAT THE DAY + NIGHT NO LONGER COME AT THEIR APPOINTED TIMES, THEN MY COVENANT WITH DAVID + THE LEVITES CAN BE BROKEN + DAVID WILL NO LONGER HAVE A DECENDENT REIGN FROM THE THRONE

WORD WEALTH

Covenant, *berit.* A covenant, compact, pledge, treaty, agreement. This is one of the most theologically important words in the Bible, appearing more than 250 times in the Old Testament. A *berit* may be made between individuals, between a king and his people, or by God with His people.[1]

The following questions will help us probe deeper. The key concept is that God is a covenant-maker:

How does Genesis 1:3–5 reveal that God is a covenant-maker?

GOD MADE THE LIGHT - DAY + THE DARK - NIGHT

Define the word "covenant" in your own words.

A PROMISE / COMMITMENT BETWEEN US + GOD

What are covenants in our society?

Do we understand the importance of covenants in our own life? Example: Malachi 2:14–16 describes the importance of the marriage covenant.

INTRODUCING THE BLOOD OF THE COVENANT
(Genesis 15:10; Leviticus 17:11)

In Genesis 15:10, we learn that God is not only the God of the covenant, but that He is the author of a specific kind of covenant, which is the blood covenant: "Then he brought all these to Him and cut them in two, down the middle, and placed each opposite the other; but he did not cut the birds in two."

Here we see the first blood-sacrifice covenant. A blood sacrifice is needed to establish a covenant. "The covenant parties then passed between the halves indicating that they were irrevocably bound together in blood. The cutting in halves of the sacrifice spoke of the end of existing lives for the sake of establishing a new bond or covenant. The sacred nature of this bond was attested to by the shedding of lifeblood. In this instance, only God passed between the pieces, indicating that it was His covenant and He would assume responsibility for its administration."[2]

In Leviticus 17:11 we learn of the power of the blood: "For the life of the flesh *is* in the blood, and I have given it to you upon the altar to make atonement for your souls; for it *is* the blood *that* makes atonement for the soul." The Scripture clearly points out, "It is the blood *that* makes atonement for the soul." The idea of a blood sacrifice appears about sixty times in the Book of Leviticus. In the New Testament, Jesus Christ is the Lamb of God who takes away our sins (John 1:29). The truth that God is a covenant-maker who restores us to a right relationship with Him through the blood of the covenant is central to the Bible. Thus, the many other religions which teach that one can have a relationship with God apart from the blood of the covenant must be false. Hinduism and Buddhism teach that a blood sacrifice is not necessary and that man and God can have a relationship through man's good works. Yet the Bible teaches that man and God can only come together through the blood of the covenant, which culminates in the death and resurrection of Jesus Christ—the blood of the Lamb.

In order for us to grasp this central biblical truth, a number of key questions must first be understood. The following questions will help us explore this pivotal truth.

First, write in your own thoughts a preliminary assessment of your perspective on the blood of the covenant. You can later weigh these comments against what you may learn as you proceed.

BLOOD MUST BE SHED FOR ATONEMENT OF OUR SINS

Why is the blood necessary for restoring a right relationship between God and man? (Lev. 17:11)

BLOOD IS OUR LIFE + MUST BE SACRIFICED FOR THE LORD

Why is it foolish for men and women to attempt to approach God through any terms other than the blood of the covenant? (Heb. 9:22)

WITHOUT THE SHEDDING OF BLOOD THERE IS NO FORGIVENESS

Do I ever attempt to approach God on the basis of my "religious works" or performance? How?

How does the blood of Jesus Christ mean freedom and liberation for me? (Gal. 1:4)

He gave His Blood For my sins, According to the will of the Father

THE GOAL OF THE BLOOD COVENANT IS A RIGHT RELATIONSHIP WITH GOD

In Isaiah 1:11, we read:

"To what purpose *is* the multitude of your sacrifices to Me?"
  Says the LORD.
"I have had enough of burnt offerings of rams
  And the fat of fed cattle.
  I do not delight in the blood of bulls,
  Or of lambs or goats."

How does the above verse tells us that God's goal is to have a pure and right relationship with us ?

It's not the sacrifice, But the attitude of our Heart

What warning to us as believers does this give about poten-
tially empty religious ceremonies in which our hearts are far away
from God? (Matt. 15:8)

THE LORD KNOWS THE STATE OF OUR
HEART

Finally, explain in your own words how the Spirit of Jesus
Christ is constantly probing our hearts and calling us to a deeper
relationship with Him (John 16:8).

HE WILL CONVICT US OF SIN, IN ORDER
TO MAKE OUR HEART RIGHT WITH HIM

King David, who is called "a man after God's own heart,"
gives us an example of this. In Psalm 51 we see how David came
to God in total transparency after he sinned with Bathsheba.
David discovered it is futile to cover up.

How does David seek to hide his sin? (2 Sam. 11:6–27)

TRY TO GET URIAH TO SLEEP WITH BATHSHEBA.
WHEN HE WOULD NOT, HE HAD HIM KILLED

What occasioned David's being forced to confront his sin?
(2 Sam. 12:15)

THE LORD STRUCK THE BABY WITH SICKNESS &
IT DIED

The key here is that David confessed his sin and did not
attempt to cover up his sin with "religious works" or fig leaves.
He does not repeat the mistake of Adam and Eve who, when

found out by God, attempted to hide, or Cain who brought his own offering to God. Here we see David taking full advantage of the blood of the covenant. He does not seek to be justified by his "works." Rather, David offers to God the sacrifice of a "broken and contrite heart."

Read Psalm 51, especially focusing on verses 1, 2, 6–13, and 17; and briefly outline the truths that David communicates.

— Confess's sin + ask for mercy
— God desires truth
" teaches wisdom
Asks God to create a clean heart
within Him.

How is transparency and honesty before God the key to spiritual vitality?

God knows our hearts + desires a pure
heart before Him

On what basis can we be confident when we come before God asking to be cleansed spiritually?

Blood of Jesus to forgive our sin

The great sin of humankind, even some in so-called Christian circles, is that we seek to justify ourselves through our own good works. Sometimes we even put on an outward show of spirituality. Yet God delights in people whose hearts are completely open before Him, hearts that are sensitive to His calling. When we come before God in praise and worship and allow the glory of His presence to create in us a tenderness and openness, then God can create a clean heart in us through His blood. The result of this openness before God is that He restores to us the joy of our salvation, without which we cannot evangelize the lost and reclaim our culture for Christ. Without restoration of the joy of salvation, we become dry bones and whitewashed tombs, as had the Pharisees (Matt. 23:27).

The blood of Jesus Christ makes it possible for us to come to God just as we are. We find cleansing and deliverance from the bondages of sin. We can receive a fresh infilling of His Spirit and have the joy of our salvation restored through the blood of the Lamb. Once we have been washed clean in His blood, then—as His bride—we begin to walk in awesome spiritual beauty and His glory radiates through us. The result is that people are won to Jesus Christ, and the power of the Adversary is destroyed. It is important, when studying these verses of scripture, that we do not just give them, in the words of the great evangelist Charles Finney, "mental assent." In other words, we are to apply them to our own hearts, not just keep them at a comfortable distance.

 ## FAITH ALIVE

Based on Psalm 51, go to the Lord in prayer in total transparency. Begin by worshiping Him and thanking Him for the light of His Holy Spirit. Ask the light of the Holy Spirit to shine into the depths of your heart. Open your heart before Him.

Allow the light of Christ to search your inward being and to create in you a clean heart. If the Lord points out anything that is unpleasing to Him, ask Him to cleanse you.

Once you have been transparent before God and asked Him to cleanse you, then ask Him *to restore to you the joy of salvation!*

THE BLOOD OF JESUS CHRIST

The Old Testament (Old Covenant) pointed the way to the blood of Jesus Christ in the New Covenant or agreement. In Hebrews 9:11–14, the apostle Paul wrote that Jesus Christ, through His own blood, entered the Most Holy Place once and for all to obtain eternal redemption. The Mosaic covenant provided animal sacrifices with an earthly altar, which was symbolic of God's eternal and heavenly altar. The New Covenant is the eternal fulfillment of God's covenant, because it destroyed the power of sin and death forever. It is freely available to anyone who will accept it.

In Ephesians 1:7 we read, "In Him we have <u>redemption through His blood</u>, the forgiveness of sins, according to the riches of His grace." The blood of the covenant culminated in redemption through Jesus Christ.

 WORD WEALTH

Redemption, *apolutrosis.* A ransom. A ransom is an amount paid so a life can be spared. The biblical meaning is a ransom paid so that there can be a release or the guarantee of the forgiveness of sins.

The question emerges, "To whom is the ransom paid?" Dr. Jack Hayford answers these questions in his CITYWIDE Bible Study. He notes that the price was the blood of Jesus and outlines four possible points of payment: "(a) Satan; (b) impersonal force of evil or death; (c) God and/or (d) the created order of things."

Dr. Hayford comments that Satan had no legal right to claim payment. Death and evil, though real, are abstract forces that cannot require payment. Thus, it was God's justice that *did* need to be satisfied, "but not," he observes, "in the sense that God was demanding payment as any human offended party might.

"The transcending issue was that what mandated justice was not God's *personal* sense of offense as much as the fact there had been a violation of the 'order of things' fundamental to His nature. This order, pre-existing man's creation, sinning, and fall, which existed because God as Creator could not beget a universe or system void of holiness, justice or their implications, had to be answered to. Only the blood of Jesus could provide that answer."

Is Christianity merely a primitive, blood-stained religion as many in our humanistic culture view it? In my own journey toward Christ, I wrestled with this viewpoint, which I shared in my book *Supernatural Faith in the New Age*: "I believed that Christianity was the 'opiate of the people.' I thought that Christians, with their barbaric religion, would prevent the 'revolution' and a 'higher consciousness' from coming to our world. Sharing Erich Fromm's point of view in *The Art of Loving*, I felt that Christianity and the belief in God was a primitive level of social development and should be transcended.

"Like many . . . , I was seduced and brainwashed to believe that there are many ways to heaven and that there is no such thing as evil incarnate or a devil. In this incorrect view of reality, I falsely believed that all evil could be attributed to ignorance or psychological problems. Basically, I subscribed to the belief that man is basically good and in the process of evolving into a higher realm of consciousness or development."

It is this perspective that is shared by many in our post-Christian culture. "Secular humanists and people who embrace Eastern mystical philosophy share a common belief in evolution either from the biological perspective of Charles Darwin or in the Hinduistic sense of reincarnation. Both ideas are based on the deception that man is moving into a higher state of being."[4]

It is here that the "rubber meets the road." Christianity is not just an archaic belief system in which men invented a blood-stained deity similar to the gods of pagan cultures, whose worship required sacrifice. The entire framework of the universe and the death force of sin unleashed into the world through man's disobedience can only be removed by a cosmic process of redemption through the sacrificial blood of Jesus Christ. This is not because God is some kind of offended being who demands retribution, but because of the real "order of things"—"a cosmic order preexisting man's creation." In other words, the universe is a complete system of holiness, love, and justice. Therefore, violation of the laws of the universe produce certain results. Those results can only be undone by the application of higher laws that find their complete expression in salvation by grace and the blood of Jesus Christ.

What this means, on the practical level, is that God designed the universe to work a certain way, just as an engineer would create an automobile engine to run on a fuel. When trying to get that car engine to run, it doesn't matter how sincere you are. If you try to put anything other than gasoline in that engine, it simply will not work. In much the same way, it is only through the blood of Jesus that our sins can be forgiven.

The questions below will help us examine more about the reality of the blood of Jesus Christ:

The price was the blood of Jesus. To whom was the ransom paid? (Rom. 3:26)

Those who have faith in Jesus

The "blood of Jesus Christ" is not just some religious terminology. Why was the blood necessary in order for redemption to occur? (Heb. 9:22)

Without the shedding of blood, there is no forgiveness

We have seen that many in our culture view references to the blood of Jesus Christ as primitive and arising from ignorance. How does the blood of Jesus Christ answer the basic problems of modern man?

FAITH ALIVE

We understand from the Bible that God is a "covenant-maker" and that He reveals Himself to us through His Word. God has revealed Himself to humankind. We can come to Him through the blood of the covenant because it is only the blood that can cleanse us from sin. Does this leave room for universalism and the belief that there are many ways to God?

No

If I am sincere and mean well, can I come to God on the basis of my sincerity?

No

Ultimately, the blood of Jesus Christ means complete liberation for me as an individual. True liberation is shedding the shackles of sin and coming out of bondage to harmful life-styles. How does the blood of the covenant and the sacrifice of Jesus Christ as the Lamb of God make it possible for me to find true freedom in life?

Blood of Jesus allows us to be forgiven of our sins

1. *Spirit-Filled Life Bible* (Nashville, TN: Thomas Nelson Publishers, 1991), 29, "Word Wealth: 17:7 covenant."

2. Ibid., 27, "Kingdom Dynamics: The First Blood Sacrifice Covenant."

3. Paul McGuire, *Supernatural Faith in the New Age* (Springdale, PA: Whitaker House, 1987), 18.

4. Ibid.

Lesson 2/Understanding the Authority of God's Word

Companioning with the theme of the blood of Christ in this study, we are looking at a second "constant" in the divine order of things—indeed, the *first*—God's Word.

Here is the link —

The Word *reveals* the need for the blood.

The blood *seals* the covenant of the Word. Both are inviolable as absolute authority:

The Word, the absolute authority of heaven's throne.

The blood, the absolute authority vanquishing sin's power.

Mankind rebels by nature against both, yet both are fundamental to the covenant of God—His Word and His blood.

Edward Mote captured this idea in the third verse and chorus of his grand old hymn "The Solid Rock":

> His oath, His covenant, His blood
> Support me in the whelming flood;
> When all around my soul gives way
> He then is all my hope and stay.

Chorus   On Christ the solid Rock I stand;
> All other ground is sinking sand.
> All other ground is sinking sand.

THE DIVINE INSPIRATION OF THE BIBLE

Second Timothy 3:16 tells us that "all scripture *is* given by inspiration of God, and *is* profitable for doctrine, for reproof, for correction, for instruction in righteousness." Today, as in years past, the truth that the Bible is divinely inspired is a key issue. On every quarter, the divine inspiration of the Bible is under attack, even within the evangelical community.

The late theologian, Dr. Francis Schaeffer, defended the issue of the divine inspiration of the Bible as the watershed issue of the Christian world. Yet major denominations that were once orthodox in their theology have embraced the flow of cultural relativism in their theology. Such issues as whether or not to make the Bible gender neutral emerge. People attempt to make God neither male nor female. In fact, the concept of God the Father is questioned, as well as issues of human sexuality.

In Luke 16:17, we read that Jesus said, "And it is easier for heaven and earth to pass away than for one tittle of the law to fail." God's Word is not subject to politically correct thinking. The truth of the Word is eternal and does not change with the passing whims of a culture.

In understanding the concept of the authority of the Bible, it is important to understand the following concepts:

Cultural relativism is a term that denotes there is no right or wrong in the universe. There are no absolutes. In other words, everything is relative. This belief system stems from the idea that there is no God and that man is the center of the universe. It is an expression of modern humanism which flows out of the existentialist thought of men, such as philosopher Jean Paul Sartre. In this view of things, absolutely everything is up for questioning, including the authority of the Scripture.

Absolutes is a term that conveys the idea that in the universe there are fixed laws that are not subject to human opinion. In other words, there is a right and a wrong. God's Word is absolute. While humanists would declare that there are no absolutes, those embracing a Judeo-Christian worldview believe that there are absolutes. There is a right and a wrong, apart from what is popular at the moment.

Final reality describes the fact that the universe and reality exist in a certain form and are not subject to popular opinion. In other words, final reality is what is real and true. The fact that Jesus Christ rose from the dead is final reality. Whether or not people choose to accept this does not alter the reality that it happened. That is final reality.

The following questions will help to give us a clearer understanding of God's Word as the final authority:

Why is the Bible the final authority in our lives? (2 Tim. 3:16)

What reason do we have to believe that there are absolutes in life? (Luke 16:17)

THE BIBLE AS THE FINAL AUTHORITY IN OUR LIVES

The Bible is to be the final authority in our lives. That means that ultimately I will choose to believe and obey what the Bible says, not the opinions of men. The reason for this belief in the Bible as the final authority is not that we choose to be religious legalists whose minds are shut from other opinions or that we are frightened of creative thinking. We believe that the Bible is the Word of God and divinely inspired. Therefore, we choose to believe it above the opinions, philosophies, and writings of men, which constantly change.

I remember studying psychology at a university. I was amazed to find that every major psychological theorist would contradict or disagree with his predecessors. Since psychology was being taught as a science, I couldn't understand why its proponents disagreed with one another. The reason they did is that their theories were based on their subjective belief systems. In contrast, the Bible is based on what God has to say and not on the opinions of men.

Psalm 119:89–91 states this truth: "Forever, O LORD, Your Word is settled in heaven. Your faithfulness *endures* to all generations; You established the earth, and it abides. They continue this day according to Your ordinances, for all *are* Your servants."

Here we see that the Bible, God's Word, is settled. It is final reality. In other words, it is true—not just in religious or spiritual matters. It is true in every area of life because God created all of life and the universe. He understands how it functions. We must get away from the notion that somehow God is intimidated by computers, technology, DNA molecules, sex, and so on. God is the Creator of humankind and the universe. He is light years beyond our present level of scientific and social development. "Our Lord is often represented as a remnant of ancient and long-dead Middle Eastern society when, in truth, he is more current and viable than anything our computers, gene splicing, high-definition television, fiber optics, and nuclear energy could imagine or produce."[1]

It is important to understand that Christianity is Truth and not a religion! God's Word is not just true because you and I choose to believe in it. It is true, because on an objective scientific basis it simply is "true." When we understand this reality, it should give us confidence in our daily living and relating to our society.

The following questions should help us to understand why God's Word is the final authority in life.

Why is it important to understand why God's Word is the final authority in life? (1 Pet. 1:25)

Define the expression "Christianity is Truth and not a religion." (John 14:6)

What does the fact that Christianity is Truth and not a religion mean to me in my everyday life? How does it give me confidence when I share my faith?

CHRISTIANITY AS TRUTH AND NOT A RELIGION

Many Christians are intimidated by science and reason. They might not admit it consciously. They feel that "maybe things like evolution are true." They are not sure that the Bible is really true when it comes to scientific, social, or historic matters. "Maybe the story of Adam and Eve, Noah and the ark, Moses' parting the Red Sea, and so on are just myths to guide us," they reason. With this thinking, these Christians do not have confidence and boldness in their faith. Their faith has been undermined, and they live on the defensive because they have never discovered for themselves the reality of the Bible's truthfulness in all areas of life.

I have met Christian parents who have been afraid to send their children to college. Individual Christians were afraid of intensely studying fields like biology, medicine, psychology, and physics for fear of losing their faith. The problem is that these people had a faith built on a religious experience that somehow had become separated from reason. They did not understand that Christianity is Truth and not a religion.

These people did not have the proper intellectual foundation for their faith. They embraced cultural relativism and a weakened view of Scripture. The importance of the Word of God as the final authority is addressed by the late Dr. Francis Schaeffer, the world-renowned theologian-philosopher, when he wrote in his book *The Great Evangelical Disaster*: ". . . the Bible is objective, absolute truth in all areas that it touches upon. And, therefore, we know Christ lived, and that Christ was raised from the dead and all the rest, not because of some subjective inner experience, but because the Bible stands as an objective absolute authority."[2]

This same issue was taken up by a meeting of the most influential theologians, evangelists, and ministers in the 1974 Lausanne Covenant. They issued this statement on the authority of God's Word: "We affirm the divine inspiration, truthfulness and authority of both Old and New Testament Scriptures in their entirety as the only written Word of God, without error in all that it affirms."

This is a key issue in individual Christian lives as well as in society at large. Dr. Schaeffer warned about undermining the authority of God's Word, even in some quarters of the Christian community, when he said:

> Here is the great evangelical disaster—the failure of the evangelical world to stand for truth as truth. There is only one word for this—accommodation: . . . The evangelical church has accommodated to the world spirit of the age. First, there has been accommodation on Scripture, so that many who call themselves evangelicals hold a weakened view of the Bible and no longer affirm the truth of all the Bible teaches—truth, not only in religious matters, but in areas of science, history and morality.[3]

The following questions will help us to integrate the truth of God's Word and the authority of the Scriptures in our lives.

How does the authority of God's Word affect my life in matters of morality? (Ps. 119:9, 11)

How does the authority of God's Word affect my life in areas of sexuality? (1 Cor. 6:19, 20)

How does the authority of God's Word affect my understanding of where man came from in relationship to the theory of evolution? (John 1:1–3)

Can I be sure that the Bible is true in areas of history, science, and morality, as well as spiritual matters? (Ps. 19:7–11)

GOD AND HIS WORD ARE ONE

The reliability and authority of God's Word are directly tied into the fact that God and His Word are one. In John 1:1–5, 14, the apostle John states that God and His Word are one and the same. Genesis 1:26 says, "Let Us make man in Our image, according to Our likeness." Here God refers to Himself as plural, which makes reference to the Deity as a *Triune Being*—God the Father, God the Son, and God the Spirit. That is why it is possible for the Scripture to say, "In the beginning was the Word, and the Word was with God, and the Word was God."

This makes the Bible unique among all other spiritual books because here God claims to be one with His Word. In fact, "God and His Word are one" also disproves the truthfulness and reliability of other so-called spiritual books, such as the *Book of Mormon*, the Hindu *Upanishads* or the *Bhagavad Gita*, the *Koran* of the Muslim religion. These books claim to be enlightened or to include special revelations. Clearly, if God and His Word are one, then He cannot contradict Himself. Therefore, these other books, which claim to be words of God, must be false because they contain things which contradict the Bible. They cannot be simultaneously true. The final proof of the authority of God's Word is the fact that Jesus Christ, who is the Word, resurrected from the dead. No other religious teacher in history made such fantastic claims. It is the resurrection of Jesus Christ, who is the Word of God, that proves once and for all the ultimate power, authority, and credence of the Bible.

In the questions below, we will further examine the truth that God and His Word are one.

What does the fact that "God and His Word are one" say about the truthfulness of the Word of God? (John 18:37)

Why is it impossible for other so-called *spiritual* books to be true?

If God and His Word are one, then what should our personal response be to anything we read in the Bible? (James 1:22)

THE AUTHORITY OF GOD'S WORD IN JUDGING ALL REVELATION

In our time, when spiritual deception is rampant, it is important that we understand the Word of God, which is the final test of the truthfulness of any spiritual revelation attributed to God. Gurus, spiritual teachers, enlightened masters, and channel guides all claim to be from God. In addition, Christians often claim to have a Word from the Lord, revelation, or prophecy. How can we be sure that it is from God?

Fortunately, God has given us a test to judge the reliability of all these things, and that is His Word. In talking about the gifts of the Holy Spirit and spiritual revelation, the apostle Paul said, "Let two or three prophets speak, and let the others judge"

(1 Cor. 14:29). In other words, we are supposed to judge all prophecy in light of the Word of God.

Within the Christian community, numerous doctrines arise that are not always biblically based. They add on to what the Bible says. In addition, people claim to have heard a word from the Lord. We are responsible to judge those things in light of the Word of God. We are not supposed to be afraid of spiritual gifts any more than we are supposed to be afraid of driving a car. However, in both cases there are rules and boundaries for our safety.

Tragically, we hear of cases in which a man or a woman claims to have heard from God that he or she should leave a present marriage partner for another person. Clearly, such an individual did not hear from God, because God specifically calls for us to be faithful in marriage. His Word has a commandment against adultery. In no case will God tell a person to do something that is contrary to His Word. This is impossible, because God cannot contradict Himself.

If we follow the Bible and believe that God and His Word are one, then we can protect ourselves from deception and error. People who are spiritually deceived are ignorant of what the Bible teaches or have chosen to ignore it.

The questions listed below will further explore this biblical truth.

How do I judge any revelation, teaching, or prophecy? (1 Cor. 14:29)

If someone claims to have a word from the Lord for me, how can I know whether it is true? (Phil. 4:8)

By what standard can I determine if any religion or spiritual teaching is true or not true? (1 John 4:3)

Is it ever possible to receive additional truth beyond what the Bible teaches? (John 14:26)

Since spiritual deception is evident all around us, should I be afraid of spiritual gifts and of the Lord's speaking to me? (John 10:27)

 ### FAITH ALIVE

Today spiritual deception is rampant in our society. Best-selling authors on national television talk shows discuss miracles, God, and Jesus. Well-known ministers and Bible teachers accuse other ministers and Bible teachers of heresy. How can I, as a believing Christian, discern the difference between truth and error?

Practical Exercise: If you wonder whether a particular teaching, prophecy, or revelation is from God, there is a simple test that you can give to yourself. Simply compare it with the Bible. In one column, write down the statement in question. In the other column, find scripture that supports it or discredits it. For example, let's examine two ideas of today and see what the Bible says about each:

1. **Reincarnation** is the belief that we live successive lives until we are perfected.

Scripture verse: Hebrews 9:27, "It is appointed for men to die once, but after this the judgment . . . ."

2. **Divine healing** is the teaching that God miraculously heals people today through faith in the changeless power of Jesus Christ.

Scripture verse: Matthew 8:16, 17, "When evening had come, they brought to Him many who were demon-possessed. And He cast out spirits with a word, and healed all who were sick, that it might be fulfilled which was spoken by Isaiah the prophet, saying, 'He Himself took our infirmities and bore our sicknesses.'"

In the first case, we see that the scripture specifically speaks *against* the idea of reincarnation. It is clear that there is absolutely no biblical basis to support the belief in reincarnation. Once we have compared this belief against the scripture, we see that they don't mix. It is either the Bible or the belief in reincarnation which is false. Since the Bible is the final authority, then we know that reincarnation is a false doctrine.

Second, we see *the scriptural foundation for divine healing*. It is important that we base our beliefs on what the Bible actually says, not on what people say that it says. Two basic errors are made in relationship to Scripture. First, there are teachings that clearly contradict what the Scripture teaches. Second, there are legitimate biblical doctrines supported by the Word of God but opposed by some because of ignorance, tradition, and prejudice. In both cases, it is on the basis of what the Bible actually says, not the opinions of men, that a doctrine's validity must be decided.

In the words of the great reformer of the church, Martin Luther: "If I profess with the loudest voice and clearest exposition every portion of truth of God except precisely that little point which the world and the Devil are at the moment attacking, I am not confessing Christ, however boldly I may be professing Christ. Where the battle rages, there the loyalty of the soldier is proved and to be steady on the battle front besides, is mere flight and disgrace if he flinches at that point . . . ."

CONCLUSION

Today, many people have serious questions regarding doctrines, teachings, and beliefs.

In all of these matters of doctrine and teaching, it is the Scripture which is to be the final authority. There is a need not only to judge everything in the light of the Scripture, but there is also a need to recognize that the body of Christ is one body. Great care must be exercised to make sure that we uphold the authority of Scripture. We cannot compromise key doctrines, such as the virgin birth of Jesus Christ and the fact of His resurrection. However, there are other beliefs that are not pivotal issues. Unity should never be built through a weakened view of Scripture. Yet, under the lordship of Jesus Christ and the authority of His Word, there is room for diverse styles of worship and emphasis. It is here we must allow the love of God to fill us that we may love all members of the body of Christ, even though they may fellowship with different denominations. Without compromising Scripture, we must avoid a nonbiblical smallness of heart and allow the Holy Spirit to develop in us an unselfish and passionate love for one another. Jesus said, "A new commandment I give to you, that you love one another; as I have loved you, that you also love one another. By this all will know that you are My disciples, if you have love for one another" (John 13:34, 35).

Write down some subjects of doctrine or church disagreement you have heard argued.

Now, what scriptural evidence do you have to support or reject each one?

Finally, how may you speak "the truth in love" (Eph. 4:15) in answering each case without becoming un-Christlike in your presentation?

1. From *Evangelizing the New Age* © 1989 by Paul McGuire, 18. Published by Servant Publications, P.O. Box 8617, Ann Arbor, Michigan 48107. Used with Permission.
2. From *The Great Evangelical Disaster* by Francis A. Schaeffer, copyright © 1984, 37. Used by permission of Good News Publishers, Crossway Books, Wheaton, Illinois 60187.
3. Ibid., 55–56.

Lesson 3/Consequences of Disobeying the Word

As a child, were you ever spanked after being hurt while you were disobeying your parents? Do you remember the shame and anger you felt?

Humankind has been involved in incidents that are far more serious ever since the beginning. We need someone to make it right again. God's Word and the Blood are His provision for us—to correct us and to cover our guilt and our shame.

GOD GIVES HIS WORD TO ADAM AND EVE

In the very beginning of time, God created Paradise for Adam and Eve to live in. The Garden of Eden was a perfect world. It answered the deepest needs of humanity. It was an eco-logically sound environment that was magnificent to look at. Adam and Eve were in perfect peace and tranquillity. Deep within the psyche of modern man is this innate drive to return to Paradise. Subconsciously, modern man knows that he was created for a better world than this one. Traffic jams, pollution, violence, war, disease, strife, poverty, shortages, and unpaid bills are not normal. They are outgrowths of the Fall of Man, which began when Adam and Eve were banished from Paradise.

Adam and Eve lived in this perfect world. The Bible calls it the Garden of Eden. Unlike many men and women today, they had a perfect relationship and lived in the very presence of God. Eden was a place of absolute harmony with waterfalls, multi-colored flowers, trees, beautiful warm skies, golden hues, and the peace and glory of God permeating the atmosphere. In addition, Adam and Eve had a perfect relationship with the animals and lit-erally "played" in Paradise. In a pure sense, modern attempts at recreating Paradise, like Club Med or hotels on the island of

Maui, would seem like ghetto streets compared to the Garden of Eden. The only thing God commanded Adam and Eve not to do is found in Genesis 2:16, 17: ". . . And the LORD God commanded the man, saying, 'Of every tree of the garden you may freely eat; but of the tree of the knowledge of good and evil you shall not eat, for in the day that you eat of it, you shall surely die.'"

Here we see that God gave man a total paradise to live in. The only thing He commanded them not to do, He did for their own good. God knew that if Adam and Eve ate of the tree of the knowledge of good and evil, a death force called "sin" would enter the human race, destroying them and their world. Far from being unreasonable, God was trying to protect Adam and Eve from certain destruction. God gave His Word to Adam and Eve in the form of a commandment to protect them and give them life. If Adam and Eve chose to disobey the Word of God, then death and destruction would result. This same principle holds true today. God gives His Word to humankind in the form of commandments for the purpose of protecting and giving life.

Keeping the above principle in mind, think of ways that disobeying God's Word results in death and destruction in the areas of marriage and human sexuality. Now write down some of the consequences of this disobedience in the lives of people you know or in society in general.

Finally, what positive impact would obeying God's Word in these areas have on our society? (Acts 17:6)

The purpose of God's giving us His Word in the form of a commandment is to bring us abundant life and to protect us. It is never God's intention to restrict us: the Word of God is always a protector and liberator.

Whenever God gives us a commandment, it is always for our own good. At times, God's commandments sometimes seem hard or difficult, especially when we want to go our own way. The commandments are always designed to produce the maximum fulfillment in our life. The root issue, in relationship to God's Word, is trusting God's goodness. When we understand the fact that God is our loving Heavenly Father and always wants the best for us, then we can have total confidence that His Word and His commandments are always for our best interest. The following questions will help us integrate this truth into our lives:

Is there ever a time that the will of God will cause me to lack any good thing or experience unfulfillment? (Phil. 4:6, 7)

Sometimes obeying God's Word means denying myself something that I want to do. Will I ever lose out by making the temporary sacrifice of obeying God's Word? (Matt. 6:18)

If God is truly a good God, should I ever fear obeying God's Word? (John 14:23)

Why is it important to obey God's Word and not the voice of society or the "crowd"? (Matt. 7:13, 14)

In Genesis 3:1–7, we are introduced into several key components regarding disobedience to the Word of God, the Fall of Man and the reality of the Devil, or the "serpent of old." After reading this scripture, answer the following questions: First, what was the specific agenda Satan had in tempting Adam and Eve to sin? (Gen. 3:1–7)

The "serpent" or the "serpent of old" is actually Satan (Rev. 12:9). In your own words, explain how Satan was able to gain dominion over humankind through tempting Adam and Eve to disobey God's Word. (Matt. 4:8–10)

How can we lose dominion in our own lives through disobeying God's Word? (Matt. 7:24–27)

At this turning point of human history, we learn several important facts about human nature, the reality of evil, and the results of disobeying God's Word.

First, we discover that there is a real evil force in the universe that had a specific agenda in tempting Adam and Eve to sin. Here in the Garden of Eden, we see Satan maneuvering for the ultimate power play, that is, the dominion of humankind, which he can only accomplish after he gets Adam and Eve to disobey God's Word.

In Revelation 12:11 we are told, "And they overcame him [Satan] by the blood of the Lamb and by the word of their testimony." In other words it is through our faith and obedience to the Word of God that we gain the power to overcome Satan (1 John 5:5). Here in the Garden of Eden, we see Satan tempting Adam and Eve to doubt and disobey the Word of God so that he can gain dominion. In reality, it is a very simple concept: Obedience to the Word of God enables us to overcome Satan; disobedience to the Word of God enables Satan to overcome us.

Other facts emerge as we read this scenario. We find out that the serpent is "cunning" and a liar. He approaches Eve with a certain amount of craftiness. The serpent gets Eve to question what God's Word actually says by causing her to question the authority and reliability of the Word of God. Satan begins his remarks with, "Has God indeed said, 'You shall not eat of <u>every</u> tree of the garden'?" Satan knew that God never said Adam and Eve could not eat of the fruit of the trees of the Garden of Eden. In Genesis 2:16, God specifically said, "And the LORD God commanded the man saying, 'Of <u>every</u> tree of the garden you may freely eat.'" Satan was lying about what God had really said. The only tree that God told them not to eat of was described in verse 17. God said, "But of the tree of the knowledge of good and evil you shall eat." Here we learn that Satan is "cunning," twists the truth and distorts what the Word of God actually says. Satan does the exact same thing today when he tempts us to disobey God's Word.

In addition, Satan directly lied to Eve when he told her, "You will not surely die" (Gen. 3:4). In Genesis 2:17 God specifically said, ". . . for in the day that you eat of it you shall surely die." The serpent not only twists the truth regarding God's Word, but he directly lies about it. In John 8:44 we learn more about Satan as the "father of lies." It is important that we under-stand that Satan is the father of lies and that God is Truth. What was the difference between what God said to Adam and Eve and what Satan said in Genesis 3:4?

How does this compare with Genesis 2:17?

After reading John 8:44, what do we learn about the very core of Satan's personality?

God and His Word are one and the same. In Psalm 119:43 it says, "And take not the word of truth utterly out of my mouth." God's Word is truth and Satan attempts to gain domin-ion in our lives through lying and twisting the truth of God's Word.

From the above passages, we see that it is the Word of God that protects us and that Satan's strategy in attempting to gain dominion in our lives is through tempting us to disobey the Word of God. The Fall of Man and Satan's temporary role as the "god of this age" came about because Adam and Eve disobeyed God's Word in the Garden of Eden. The root cause of all of our problems today and the introduction of the death force or sin into the human race happened because God's Word was disobeyed.

We need to understand how disobedience to the Word of God always brings negative consequences and why Satan will always tempt us to disobey God's Word through lies and twisting the truth. The following questions will examine this truth more completely:

How did Satan lie to Adam and Eve in the Garden of Eden? (Gen. 3:4)

How did Satan twist the truth in the Garden of Eden? (Gen. 3:1)

How does Satan lie to us today? Give some specific examples. (1 John 2:16)

How has Satan lied to you in your own life?

What were the results for Adam and Eve after they disobeyed the Word of God?

Was there anything true in what Satan told Adam and Eve in the Garden of Eden? (Gen. 3:1, 4, 5)

THE FALL OF MAN AND THE NEED FOR A COVERING

When Adam and Eve disobeyed the Word of God, sin entered the human race; and the Fall of Man resulted. Read this account in Genesis 3:7–13 and answer the following questions.

Write in your own words what happened to Adam and Eve after they ate of the forbidden fruit.

How did this affect their spiritual natures? (Gen. 3:8)

Immediately after Adam and Eve ate of the forbidden fruit, their spiritual natures were short-circuited. Eating of the tree of the knowledge of good and evil produced a total change in their consciousness. Adam and Eve, who had walked in complete peace and joy in the presence of God, now felt an intense separation from Him. For the first time fear entered their minds and hearts. Their innocence was lost, and they knew they were naked, not just physically but spiritually. Their immediate response was to attempt to cover their nakedness through their own effort, so they sewed "fig leaves together and made themselves coverings" (Gen. 3:7).

How did disobedience to the Word of God through the deception of Satan cause fear to enter the human race? (Gen. 3:10)

Notice what happened to Adam and Eve when they heard the sound of the Lord God walking: their hearts no longer rejoiced; instead, they felt both fear and shame. Their supernatural relationship with God had become polluted and ugly, so they attempted to hide their nakedness with "fig leaves." But this man-made effort toward self-covering was ridiculous because they were not just naked physically but spiritually. When God asked them, "Who told you that you were naked?" He did not have to be told that they had eaten of the tree of the knowledge of good and evil. The very atmosphere of the Garden of Eden had changed. God instantly knew when they had eaten of the fruit because He could sense the separation of Adam and Eve from His intimate presence and He understood the devastating destruction that sin would bring about.

Why was it foolish for Adam and Eve to stand before God with "fig leaves"? (Gen. 3:7)

How does this compare with other self-efforts to get close to God? (Eph. 2:8, 9)

Why was it only through the blood of Jesus Christ that the death and destruction unleashed by Adam and Eve could be undone? (Rom. 5:14–19)

In Genesis 3:21 we read, "Also for Adam and his wife the LORD God made tunics of skin, and clothed them." Here we see that God provided a covering for them through the sacrifice of innocent animals. The sacrifice of innocent animals was a fore-shadowing of the blood of the covenant. God was covering the nakedness and sin of Adam and Eve through a substitutionary sacrifice. Only God could undo the power of sin as He would later do through the blood of Jesus Christ.

Adam and Eve's disobedience to the word of God caused death and destruction to enter the human race. Satan gained do-minion over humankind through Adam and Eve's disobedience.

However, God began a plan to restore humankind's dominion over the planet through the blood of the covenant.

How does disobeying the Word of God cause the death force of sin to become operative in our lives and cause us to lose power? (Gen. 2:17)

Think of areas in your own life in which you have disobeyed God, and write down the ways you have actually lost control and power due to disobedience. For example, disobedience in the area of tithing and giving to the Lord's work will diminish your resources. In other words, by holding onto your money you actually end up losing the blessing that God had intended for you.

Lesson 4/Two Directions for Humankind

Many of us come to believe in God only after coming to "the end of our rope." We struggle and fail and then turn to God. We think we know better than God how things should be, until we surrender our agenda for His. We say, "O.K. You win. I believe that You love me and that You have things figured out better than I do. I put my trust in You." (See Is. 55:8, 9.)

The following Bible story illustrates the difference between two men—one who accepted God's way and one who thought he knew better.

The "victim" in this story is still saying something to us today (Heb. 11:4). Let's find out what it is.

THE STORY OF CAIN AND ABEL
(Genesis 4:1–10)

Genesis 4:1–10 relates the account of Cain murdering his brother Abel. In Genesis 4:3–5 we read, "And in the process of time it came to pass that <u>Cain brought an offering of the fruit of the ground to the LORD. Abel also brought of the firstborn of his flock and of their fat</u>. And the LORD respected Abel and his offering, but He did not respect Cain and his offering. And Cain was very angry, and his countenance fell."

Here we see that Cain approached God on the basis of his own works and self-effort. In distinct contrast, Abel approached God through the blood of the covenant. Earlier in Genesis 3:21, we read how God made tunics of animal skin for Adam and Eve in the first blood covering. God had already established the blood of the covenant. It stated that after the Fall, man could only come to God through a blood sacrifice. In addition, God had already rejected the self-made covering of fig leaves by Adam and Eve. Since this information had been passed on to Cain and Abel, Cain had no excuse in violating the blood covenant.

It is important that we understand why Cain's offering from his vegetable garden was wrong. In the two questions below we can examine the difference between Cain's offering and Abel's.

Why was Abel's offering acceptable to God? (Gen. 4:4)

Why was Cain's offering rejected by God? (Gen. 4:3, 5)

At the dawn of history, the account in Genesis of Cain and Abel represents the two different philosophical streams of humankind—(1) those who obey the Word of God and approach God through the blood covenant (Abel) and (2) those who disobey the Word of God and attempt to come to God on their own terms or ideas (Cain). Make no mistake about it: humanistic philosophies and all man-made religions come out of the philosophical flow of Cain.

The living God of the universe went to great lengths to communicate with humankind the need for a blood covenant. This communication has bridged centuries of civilization and has been confirmed with powerful miracles that found their full expression in the death and resurrection of Jesus Christ in real space-time history. Therefore, men and women are really without any excuse when they choose to reject God's chosen method of salvation by faith in Jesus Christ through the blood covenant.

Modern humanism, with all its emphasis on humanly energized and resourced programs of self-esteem and self-actualization, is really the religion of Cain who offered the fruit of his own work to God. Of course, there is nothing wrong with "self-esteem" or purposeful pursuit of life's goals when it flows from a right relationship with God. It is interesting to note that, in response to God's rejecting Cain's offering, Cain became very angry and murdered his brother Abel. Ultimately, those who have come to God with the fruit of their own offering become angry and begin to persecute those who have come to God through the blood. This is why, throughout history, both Christians and Jews have been persecuted. It also explains why, in our time, some who have embraced humanism have embarked on a campaign to eradicate Christianity from our culture. It is the hatred of Cain expressed in contemporary terms. Men and women will either surrender to the lordship of Jesus Christ through the blood covenant or they will be ruled by the powers of darkness because of their rejection of God's way.

It is important that we understand the spiritual root of all false religions, including the religion of humanism. Despite its false pretenses at being a science, humanism is nothing more than a false religion with its own doctrines and its own patron saints. It requires faith that is separated from reason by its followers as well as the same kind of blind allegiance that any other cult would demand. In understanding this false spiritual dynamic, we might inquire:

In what ways do humanism, the New Age, and false religions come out of the philosophical flow of Cain? (Jude 11)

In what ways do some people who embrace humanism, the New Age, and false religions maintain antagonism toward Christianity?

CAIN: THE SPIRITUAL FATHER OF HUMANISM AND FALSE RELIGIONS

When Cain deliberately rejected God's provision through the blood covering and came to God on his own terms, he became the spiritual father of all those who, throughout history, have rejected God's plan of salvation. This philosophical flow, stemming from Cain, was the spiritual force behind ancient Babylonian occult religions and Hinduism which began along the banks of the Ganges and Indus rivers in northern India as early as 2000 to 1000 B.C. Hinduism flowed into Buddhism, which was also founded in India by Siddhartha Gautama (the Buddha) who lived between 560 and 480 B.C. It was the Buddha who developed the *Noble Eight-fold Path* to God which listed eight techniques that consisted of: (1) right belief, (2) right aspiration, (3) right speech, (4) right action, (5) right occupation, (6) right effort, (7) right thought, and (8) right meditation. In a nutshell, Buddha's *Noble Eight-fold Path* is a rigorous program of self-effort. This was the mistake of Cain. He should have come to God on God's terms through the blood of the covenant. (For further reading, see *Evangelizing the New Age*, by Paul McGuire.)

The vast majority of the world's religions flow from Hinduism and Buddhism. Religions, such as Muhammadanism, stem from the teachings of the self-proclaimed prophet named Muhammad. He also prescribed a program of religious works, even though he borrowed heavily from the Bible. Finally, modern humanism evolved and gained momentum through French existentialists such as Albert Camus (1913–1960) and Jean-Paul Sartre (1905–1980). Basically, humanism suggests that there is no God and man must save himself. It also comes out of the flow of Cain because it is a rejection of God's truth in favor of a man-made religion where man becomes the center of the universe. In our time, humanism has produced pessimism and despair among an entire generation. The result has been that humanism has now flowed into the mysticism of the New Age Movement.

Other historic religions are renewing their influence upon our day. By money and media, traditional religious systems as well as cults are spreading around the world and popularizing human philosophies of "salvation" without Christ or the Cross.

Comparisons such as those above are not born of hateful

attitudes toward other religions. Rather they are concerns over (1) the insufficiency of systems sincerely seeking God but tragically missing Him, and (2) the need to know the difference so that we may both steadfastly and sensitively reach out to the lost of our generation. Thus, let us see clearly the roots of these systems.

The following questions will help us to understand how the offering of Cain relates to these developments.

Compare Buddha's *Noble Eight-fold Path* with the offering of Cain. (Eph. 2:8, 9)

How is the basic mistake of humanism similar to Cain's mistake? (Rom. 1:21)

What is the fundamental issue at stake? (1 Cor. 1:25)

Since Muhammadanism is a nonbiblical means of relating to God, how is it similar to the offering of Cain?

ABEL IS THE SPIRITUAL FOREFATHER OF ALL THOSE WHO SEEK TO BE JUSTIFIED BY FAITH

In sharp contrast to all those who attempt to come to God on their own terms, there are those who seek to come to God on His terms or through the blood of the covenant. They come out of the flow of obedience to God exemplified by Abel. He obeyed God and came to Him through a blood covenant in which he offered God the firstborn of his flock. Throughout the Bible, we find that men and women are justified before God through their faith in God's promise and not through their own works. In Romans 4:2, 3 we read, "For if Abraham was justified by works, he has *something* to boast about, but not before God. For what does the Scripture say? 'Abraham believed God, and it was <u>accounted</u> to him for righteousness.'"

 WORD WEALTH

Accounted, *logidzomai.* Compare "logistic" and "logarithm." Numerically, to count, compute, calculate, sum up. Metaphorically, to consider, reckon, reason, deem, evaluate, value. *Logidzomai* finalizes thought, judges matters, draws logical conclusions, decides outcomes, and puts every action into a debit or credit position.[1]

It is important that we understand how God's law of putting men right before Himself actually works. Nowhere does the Bible teach that by performing religious duties, men and women can earn their righteousness! This makes the teaching of Christianity completely unique among every other religion in the world. Muhammadanism teaches that its believers must adhere to a strict set of commandments and religious practices. Many cults teach their followers that they must complete many religious programs in order to earn their righteousness before God. The New Age Movement, based on ancient Hinduism and Buddhism, teaches that we must work off our *karma.*

However, the Bible teaches something completely different. The apostle Paul writes about King David, who committed both murder and adultery (Rom. 4:5–8):

> But to him who does not work but believes on Him who justifies the ungodly, his faith is accounted for righteousness, just as David also describes the blessedness of the man to whom God imputes righteousness apart from works:

> "Blessed are those whose lawless deeds are forgiven,
>   And whose sins are covered;
> Blessed *is the* man to whom the LORD shall not
>   impute sin."

King David was called "a man after God's own heart." Yet he committed murder and adultery. David paid a heavy price for those sins in his life. However, through the blood and his faith in God's ability to make him righteous, he was made righteous before God. God hates sin. We will reap the consequences of those sins that we commit, in terms of the emotional, psychological, and physical debris that sin brings. However, if we repent and choose to accept God's gift of righteousness in Jesus Christ, we can enjoy right standing with God.

In Romans 1:17 the Scripture says, "For in it [the gospel of Christ] the righteousness of God is revealed from faith to faith; as it is written, 'The just shall live by faith.'" This is the way Abel came to God—on the basis of his faith in God's blood covenant and not on the merit of his own works.

Finally, in Isaiah 64:6 we read the words: "But we are all like an unclean *thing,*/And all our righteousnesses are like filthy rags."

This means that *all* of our attempts to make ourselves holy and pure before God are like filthy rags to God. God is not interested in our religious duties and good works as a means of our attempting to earn "heavenly brownie points" with Him. God does want us to love people and do good things. However, these things that we do, in terms of ministry and good works, do not earn us "points" with God. If we are reading the Bible, tithing, praying, and doing good works because we are trying to move up some invisible scale of spirituality, then we are missing the point. All those things are important for our spiritual growth, and they benefit us. But they do not earn God's approval! God already totally approves of us because of our faith in what Jesus Christ has done.

The questions below will enable us to understand this truth of God's righteousness based on faith:

Is there anything I can do to get God to "like me" more? (Heb. 11:6)

As a believer, if I commit a sin and confess that sin before God, am I any less holy and pure? (1 John 1:9)

If a person wants to accept Jesus Christ, should we encourage him or her to clean up his or her life before accepting Jesus as Savior? (Matt. 11:28)

Should a person stop sinning before he or she can ask Christ into their lives? (Matt. 1:21)

If a person is bound by different habits, even after he or she accepts Jesus Christ, is it key that he or she stop doing those things before asking God for baptism in the Holy Spirit? (John 1:33) How would you counsel such an individual?

 ### FAITH ALIVE

It is vitally important that we understand the powerful biblical truth that "the just shall live by faith." When ministering to people about the gospel, we should always remember that God will meet them exactly where they are and they *never* have to clean themselves up first. The Holy Spirit works inside a person to clean him or her from the inside out, rather than that individual's trying to clean up in order to please God.

Listed below are some specific real-life situations that we may encounter as we attempt to minister the life of Jesus Christ to people. Apply the great truth of God's righteousness based on faith to each situation.

SITUATION ONE

1. We meet an individual who is "living with someone" outside of marriage. How should we approach leading them to Jesus Christ?

Answer: We should always invite people to accept Jesus Christ right where they are in life. Certainly, God does not approve of a sexual relationship outside of marriage. However, first the individual must receive a new nature, which only Christ can give. After that priority has been met, the biblical truths of sexual purity can be explained.

SITUATION TWO

2. A believing Christian has a smoking habit. Should this Christian stop the habit of smoking in order to "prepare to receive" the baptism of the Holy Spirit?

Answer: No. The person may need the spiritual power and deliverance that the baptism of the Holy Spirit brings in order to become free from the smoking habit. The infusion of spiritual power that the baptism of the Holy Spirit brings is deliverance from sin and habits that bind that person.

SPIRITUAL PRINCIPLE

It is Jesus Christ who purifies and gives us the power to become victorious. Christianity is not a matter of our trying to be holy and doing good works. Christianity is about a personal relationship with Jesus Christ. We become holy and minister good works not as a means of trying to become righteous, but rather, as the power of Jesus Christ fills us, we naturally become more like Him.

Reflection: Having dealt with the theme of righteousness by faith alone, how would you apply this truth to your own life?

How would you apply what you have studied to your personal relationship with people you work with or live around who don't know Christ?

How would this truth affect your approach in witnessing to them?

1. *Spirit-Filled Life Bible* (Nashville, TN: Thomas Nelson, 1991), 1693, "Word Wealth: 4:3 accounted."

Lesson 5/The Blood of Jesus—A New and Living Way

How frustrating when searching for an address to come to a dead-end street with no way through to the other side, or to feel the panic rise in your throat when you've become lost in a fun house maze. It's not funny, is it?

Jesus came to make a way where there was no way—no approach to Father God in a loving and worshipful relationship, and no path to meaningful and victorious living.

Let's look at what Jesus has done to make a way for us.

JESUS CHRIST, THE NEW COVENANT AND THE BLOOD OF THE LAMB

Hebrews 9:9–15 describes how Jesus Christ is High Priest of a New Covenant. Throughout the Old Testament, God instituted what was called the Mosaic Covenant, with animal sacrifices provided to offer temporary covering for man's sin and guilt. These animal sacrifices constituted the first blood covenant of the Old Testament—the Old Covenant. These animal sacrifices were conducted annually at a tabernacle that was symbolic of God's eternal altar.

Read Hebrews 9:9–15, and be reminded.

The following questions will help us to probe the reality of the New Covenant:

How is the New Covenant different from the Old Covenant? (Heb. 8:6; 9:15)

Why were the Old Testament sacrifices of animals of limited value? (Heb. 10:4)

In the Levitical sacrifices, the worshipers were not made perfect. Animal sacrifices had to be repeated yearly. The ancient tabernacle had to be sanctified by the blood of these animals. The Old Testament sacrifices were merely earthly copies of the heavenly altar.

What both the Old Testament and the New Testament teach us is that the universe and the throne room of God are not constructed randomly. God is a totally holy Being whose very presence cannot tolerate sin. The holy presence of God literally destroys sin with a burning, purifying fire. Obviously since man has been contaminated by sin, he would be destroyed instantly in the presence of God. God solved this problem through the blood of Jesus Christ. The blood of Jesus Christ actually takes away the sin from human beings so that God's presence can visit them without destroying them. It makes it possible for us to enter into the throne room of God, because it totally purifies us and redeems us from sin. In Hebrews 10:19–22 we read:

> Therefore, brethren, having boldness to enter the Holiest by the blood of Jesus, by a new and living way which He consecrated for us, through the veil, that is, His flesh, and *having* a High Priest over the house of God, let us draw near with a true heart in full assurance of faith, having our hearts sprinkled from an evil conscience and our bodies washed with pure water.

Why can we have confidence and boldness to go directly into the presence of God? (Heb. 10:19)

How does the blood of Jesus make a new and living way for us to go to God? (Heb. 10:20)

How does the blood of Jesus Christ give us direct access to God in a way that is completely unique among the world's religious systems? (Heb. 9:12–14)

This passage of scripture (Heb. 10:19–22) declares the stark contrast between the message of Jesus Christ and every other religion on the face of the earth. The millions of people who flock to Mecca, the hundreds of thousands who bathe in the holy river in India, the spiritual pilgrims who climb the heights of the Himalayan mountains in search of answers, the zealous Scientologists who spend hundreds of thousands of dollars to go up the "bridge" of enlightenment to experience being "clear" do not understand the liberating truth. Because of the blood of Jesus Christ we now have direct access to God. We can enter into the very presence of God boldly with full assurance because of the blood of Jesus Christ.

Although at face value this truth may seem so simple, it is precisely what makes the message of the gospel radically different from any of the religious systems on the face of the earth. The majority of religions and spiritual systems recognize that man is separated from God, but they have no real means of dealing with the problem. The blood of Jesus Christ actually deals with the sin problem by removing it from our lives.

A New Covenant

In Hebrews 8:7–13 we see the power of the New Covenant at work. The first covenant was an external covenant that set a standard by the Law with no real power to keep it. The New Covenant is a covenant of God's grace whereby the Holy Spirit is released to transform the inner beings of God's children. Therefore, obedience to God's laws is not done through an outward adherence to a list of commandments but rather through an inner change produced by a new nature. Read Hebrews 8:7–13, and consider the following questions:

How does the blood of Jesus Christ make it possible for God to put His laws in our minds and hearts? (Heb. 8:10)

How is Jesus Christ the new and living way? (Heb. 10:19, 20)

How does this new and living way differ from the old way? (Heb. 9:9–14)

How does this new and living way make it possible for us to experience victory in our lives? (Heb. 10:21, 22)

Why is the reality of Jesus Christ's being the new and living way cause for celebration? (Heb. 10:14–17)

The blood of Jesus Christ made it possible for us to be cleansed of our sins and enjoy intimate fellowship with God. This intimacy of relationship with God was impossible under the first covenant. The ministry of Jesus Christ released by His blood allows the Holy Spirit of God to place the laws of God in our hearts and minds. Thus, through the blood of Jesus Christ and receiving forgiveness for our sins by accepting Jesus Christ into our lives and becoming "born-again," we receive a new nature. The Fall of Man is reversed in our hearts, and the powers of sin and death are broken. The intimate fellowship our real space-time genetic ancestors Adam and Eve enjoyed in the Garden of Eden is restored.

Our minds and hearts become renewed and our spiritual natures are regenerated by the blood of the Lamb. This is the new and living way that is referred to in Hebrews 10:20. This new and living way means that what happened in the Garden of Eden when Satan tempted Adam and Eve is now undone. The curse is broken, and God has provided a new and living way for each of us to return to God. That way is through the blood of Jesus Christ. In John 14:6 Jesus Christ said, "I am the way, the truth, and the life. No one comes to the Father except through Me."

Jesus Christ is the way to God—the new and living way! What this means is that the blood of Jesus Christ restores the relationship with Himself that our ancestors Adam and Eve had in the Garden of Eden.

THE NEW AND LIVING WAY IN PRACTICAL TERMS

It would be a great tragedy to simply discuss the reality of Jesus Christ's being the new and living way in merely "spiritual" terms. The profound reality of Jesus Christ, as the new and living way, has nothing less than revolutionary impact upon every aspect of our lives. What modern psychotherapy, behavioral scientists, drugs and techniques like meditation cannot do is essentially change human nature. Men and women are often caught on a treadmill of techniques and recovery programs. Yet the blood of Jesus Christ truly has the power to set free. Popular psychologist R. D. Laing coined the term "knots" in describing the quandary human relationships, in our time, can often result in. The blood of Jesus Christ speaks powerfully to these problems.

We need to understand that the root of all of our problems today is what happened in the Garden of Eden centuries earlier. When man's spiritual nature died and spiritual darkness invaded the human consciousness and spirit, all the myriad problems within the human personality (for example, fear, anxiety, guilt, anger, bitterness, and all resultant psychological disorders that stem from them) began to flow out of man's sinful nature.

The fact that through the blood of Jesus Christ, which is the new and living way, we can once again experience an intimate relationship with God profoundly affects these problems. It must be understood that Adam and Eve did not have any of these problems, because they were fully alive, spiritually. God's presence filled and saturated their beings. Once that Holy presence of God was removed through sin, those problems became manifest. Now we can "enter the Holiest by the blood of Jesus Christ by a new and living way which He consecrated for us, through the veil, that is, His flesh" (Heb. 10:19, 20).

Jesus said, "*Your* heavenly Father [will] give the Holy Spirit to those who ask Him!" (Luke 11:13). In John 20:22 we read,

"He breathed on *them* and said to them, 'Receive the Holy Spirit.'" See also Acts 1:8. Here we see that through Jesus Christ—the new and living way—the promise of the Holy Spirit is released. The intimate presence and fellowship that Adam and Eve knew with God in Eden is restored. Once again mankind can be filled and saturated with the holy presence and glory of God. When the Holy Spirit of God is released upon men and women in a baptism of His healing glory, the problems manifested by man's sin nature begin to diminish and will progressively be overcome as faith's pathway of victory is learned.

The new and living way, made possible by the blood of Jesus Christ, dissolves the "knots" in human relationships. Physical and mental healing, at every dimension, is made possible by the release of God's presence and glory. In a nutshell, behavioral therapy, biofeedback, hypnotherapy, visualization, drugs, and mere techniques fail man. When God's glory and presence are released through the new and living way, which is the blood of Jesus, man is spiritually resurrected and restored to right relationship with God.

The presence of God within us through the Holy Spirit puts God's laws in our hearts and minds because we become regenerated through the Word of God and the Holy Spirit, who is made available to us through the blood of the Lamb. The new and living way is both powerful and profound because the release of God's glory within the temples of our human personality is as awesome as the *Shekinah* glory of God, which filled the Old Testament temple.

In 2 Chronicles 7:1–3 we read the account of how Solomon dedicated the temple with the blood of animal sacrifices and how God's glory filled the temple:

> When Solomon had finished praying, fire came down from heaven and consumed the burnt offering and the sacrifices; and the glory of the LORD filled the temple. And the priests could not enter the house of the LORD, because the glory of the LORD filled the LORD's house. When all the children of Israel saw how the fire came down, and the glory of the LORD on the temple, they bowed their faces to the ground on the pavement, and worshiped and praised the LORD, *saying*:

"For *He is* good,
     For His mercy *endures* forever."

If the Old Testament animal sacrifices, in the first covenant, could release the glory of God so powerfully that the priests could not enter the temple because the glory of the Lord filled the house, think of how much more powerfully the glory and presence of God is released in the temples of our human personalities through the new and living way, the blood of Jesus Christ. God wants His glory to fill the house of our personalities in an overflowing measure. When we understand the provision that God made for us in the new and living way, through the blood of Jesus Christ, then we can open ourselves to this divine resource, and the glory of the Lord will fill our house.

Reflection: Why does God want His glory to fill the "house" of our personalities in overflowing measure?

How will being filled regularly with the presence and glory of God affect our everyday lives?

How does the provision that God made for us through the blood of Jesus Christ make it possible for us to experience God's glory at work in our lives?

FAITH ALIVE

Apply the great truth, Hebrews 10:19, 20. Go boldly to God through the new and living way, which is the blood of Jesus. Spend some time in prayer with God and draw near to Him in full assurance of faith. Begin by praising and worshiping Him. Ask Him to fill you with the glory of His presence. Ask Him to fill you freshly with His Holy Spirit.

Allow the presence of God to overflow your personality and praise Him for filling the empty places or problems of your life with divine glory. Rejoice in His magnificent presence and spend some time worshiping Him. Allow Him to bathe you in His light and glory and let any oppression in your life be completely lifted. Go ahead! Praise Him!

Lesson 6/The Power of God's Word

We have just seen that Jesus is THE Way (John 14:6)—a new and living way (Heb. 10:20). He is also THE Word (John 1:1, 14). In a sense, how we regard Jesus Christ and how we regard God's Word are the same.

Harold Hill in *How to Live Like a King's Kid* referred to the Bible as the "Manufacturer's Handbook." We have heard it said, "If all else fails, follow directions." God has given us a powerful and practical resource in His Word "that the man of God may be complete, thoroughly equipped for every good work" (2 Tim. 3:17).

GOD'S WORD IS RELIABLE AND PRACTICAL

The foundational constant in life is the authority and reliability of God's Word. People change, nations rise and fall, economies falter, and physical bodies decay. Yet, in the midst of earthly chaos, God's Word and the promises it contains are unshakable. Every believer in Jesus Christ will inevitably face trials in this life. First Peter 4:12, 13 states, "Beloved, do not think it strange concerning the fiery trial which is to try you, as though some strange thing happened to you; but rejoice to the extent that you partake of Christ's sufferings, that when His glory is revealed, you may also be glad with exceeding joy."

Each of us will, sooner or later, face the furnace of life's adversities. None of us are immune from trials, temptation, or difficulty. Yet it is at these moments that we have the divine opportunity to stand on the Word of God.

It is at these times that we need to wage spiritual warfare and "take the helmet of salvation, and the sword of the Spirit, which is the word of God" (Eph. 6:17). When Jesus Christ reminded Peter in Luke 22:31, "Simon, Simon! Indeed, Satan has asked for you, that he may sift *you* as wheat," the Lord was reminding all of us that we have an Adversary. Many of life's trials and problems are brought on by a very real and unseen enemy who wishes to destroy us.

It is the Word of God that is the powerful "sword of the Spirit." In Psalm 119:89 we are told, "Forever, O LORD, Your word is settled in heaven." God's Word is the most powerful force in the universe. We need to apply its power to every area of life. The challenge for us as individual believers in Jesus Christ is to integrate the truth of the Scriptures into the real world and translate the Bible to everyday life. In the book *Evangelizing the New Age*, these issues are addressed:

> The Bible speaks to political issues, science, law, sexuality, marriage, business, sociology, history, literature, and a wide spectrum of life. I cannot tell you how many churches I have visited where the minister seemed to be speaking from the stratosphere with theological phrases and words like redemption, sanctification, eschatology, millennialism, regeneration, and so on. Even well-meaning sermons seem to float like clouds above the heads of the people. Many times I have said to myself, "What does all this mean to my life in the real world? How do the words of Jesus Christ and the Bible apply to the nitty-gritty details of my life?" Let us ask ourselves how the Bible speaks to these needs:
>
> —My marriage is breaking up.
>
> —My boss hates me.
>
> —My career is going nowhere.
>
> —I am depressed.
>
> —Nightmares torment me.
>
> —I have unpaid bills.
>
> —My sexual desire is strong, and I'm single (or divorced).
>
> —I want to get ahead at work.

—My husband has a drinking problem and is not a Christian.

—I have homosexual desires.

—I am a Christian and I have a problem with pornography.

—I am addicted to drugs.

—I am a victim of child abuse.

—I am an adult child of an alcoholic and I can't break free from the psychological bondage.

—I feel that I have so much potential in life, but I can't seem to unlock it.

—I want to get over my fears and phobias.

—I'm lonely, and all my Christian friends just quote scriptures at me.

—I feel like a failure.[1]

The key here is to learn how to apply the power of God's Word into the practicality of life. Subtly, without recognizing it, believers in Jesus Christ have a tendency to make biblical truth *religious* rather than *real*. Yet, it is in the acid test of reality that our faith has the chance to grow and develop. In fact, our loving Heavenly Father will allow real life experiences to come into our lives as divine opportunities for growth. And we will find many occasions when we simply will come to the end of our own resources. It is in these places that we will learn the power of the promises of God's Word. The following questions will help us to integrate these truths into our lives:

How does the power of God's Word apply to where I live right now in my life with the various situations I face? (Matt. 4:4)

What does it mean that the Word of God is the "sword of the Spirit"? (Eph. 6:17)

How can I use this "sword of the Spirit" in the challenges that life brings me and against the powers of darkness? (Eph. 6:12)

THE WORD OF GOD IS LIVING AND POWERFUL

In Hebrews 4:12 the apostle Paul writes, "For the word of God *is* living and powerful, and sharper than any two-edged sword, piercing even to the division of soul and spirit, and of joints and marrow, and is a discerner of the thoughts and intents of the heart." Once again, we see the reference that the word of God is a sword and that it is powerful. Not only does it move into the depths of our being when we hear or read it, but it contains the power to transform our world internally and externally.

 WORD WEALTH

Powerful, *energes.* Comparable in meaning to the English word "energetic." Denotes something at work, active, and effective.[2]

Not only is God's Word powerful, but the term for "word" in Hebrews 4:12 is the Greek word *logos*.

 WORD WEALTH

Word, *logos.* A transmission of thought, communication, a word of explanation, an utterance, discourse, divine revelation, talk, statement, instruction, an oracle, divine promise, divine doctrine, divine declaration. Jesus is the living *logos* (John 1:1); the Bible is the written *logos* (Heb. 4:12); and the Holy Spirit utters the spoken *logos* (1 Cor. 2:13).[3]

The word *logos* in Hebrews 4:12 contrasts with the word *rhema,* which is a specific word spoken or given. Speaker and international Bible teacher Roy Hicks defines the word *rhema* as "the single promise or promises the Holy Spirit may bring to our mind from the Word of God. When facing a situation of need, trial, or difficulty, the promises of God may become a *rhema* to you; that is, a weapon of the Spirit."[4]

 WORD WEALTH

Word, *rhema.* That which is said or spoken, an utterance, in contrast to *logos,* which is the expression of a thought, a message, a discourse. *Logos* is the message; *rhema* is the communication of the message. In reference to the Bible, *logos* is the Bible in its entirety; *rhema* is a verse from the Bible. The meaning of *rhema,* in distinction from *logos,* is illustrated in Ephesians 6:17, where the reference is not to the Scripture as a whole, but to that portion which the believer wields as a sword in a time of need.[5]

Think of ways that specific promises of God have been a *rhema* in your life. Write down three promises of God from His Word that have given you hope and victory in times of personal trial.

1.

2.

3.

How did the *rhema* of God's Word give you the courage and hope to go on in the midst of difficulty?

GOD AND HIS WORD ARE ONE

In John 1:1, 14, we read that God and His Word are one. Jesus Christ is the Word become flesh. When we read, study, meditate, or hear God's Word, we are receiving living energy into our beings and the very presence of God Himself. The result is regeneration and transformation—God's Word produces life.

How does the fact that God and His Word are one affect my reading and studying of the Bible? (Ps. 138:2; John 1:1, 18)

If God and His Word are one, what does that say about other religions, which teach ideas that are contrary to His Word? (John 14:6)

Is it possible for any religious teaching, guru, spiritual teacher, or book to be of God if it contradicts what the Bible says? (1 John 4:6)

GOD CREATED THE UNIVERSE AND MANKIND THROUGH HIS WORD

In Genesis, we see that humankind and the created order were not the result of evolutionary randomness or some kind of cosmic "big bang." Instead, the Word of God created both humankind and planet Earth in God's image with its rich, created wonders. The stars flickering in the night sky, the sun rising and setting in its brilliant hues, the uniqueness of every man and woman alive, are all the result of the energy and power of God's Word in action (read Gen. 1:1, 3, 6, 9, 11, 26).

It bears repeating to say Christianity is Truth and not a religion. The Word of God is final reality. It is what is real, beyond the opinions or pseudo-scientific theories of any culture or age. Civilizations rise and fall. Yet God's Word stands forever.

THE IMPORTANCE OF READING, STUDYING, AND MEDITATING IN GOD'S WORD

Since God's Word is so total, comprehensive, powerful, and life-changing, it is vital that we read, study, and meditate on it on a daily basis. In Psalm 119:105 we read, "Your Word *is* a lamp to my feet and a light to my path." God's Word is an actual light upon our pathway in life. When we read it and study it, the Word illuminates the issues of our life. In Joshua 1:8 we read about the Word of God as the secret to success in life. That verse describes three things we must do with the Word of God in order to have success in life. They are as follows:

1. Speak the Word of God. ("This Book of the Law shall not depart from your mouth.")

2. Meditate in the Word of God. ("You shall meditate in it day and night.")

3. Do what the Word of God says. ("Observe to do according to all that is written in it.")

Describe how you can apply these three principles in your life:

1. Speaking God's Word.

2. Meditating in God's Word.

3. Doing God's Word.

The three keys to success in life are all related to the power of God's Word. First, it is imperative that we speak what the Word of God says about us, the situations we face, and the blessing of the Word to the people we meet. In recent years, there has been much controversy regarding what has been called "positive confession" or what some of its critics have called "name it and claim it." It is true that there have been some who took a legitimate biblical truth regarding speaking God's Word and went off on a tangent. Yet the fact remains that it is the Word of God that commands us to "speak the Word." ("This Book of the Law shall not depart from your mouth.")

When we speak contrary to God's Word or speak negatively, we literally block the flow of God's power moving in our lives. There is a powerful biblical truth here. When we speak God's Word, a creative force of blessing and power is released. This truth is further amplified in Mark 11:23, which records Jesus' words, "For assuredly, I say to you, whoever says to this mountain, 'Be removed and be cast into the sea,' and does not doubt in his heart, but believes that those things he says will be done, he will have whatever he says."

Speaking God's Word should not cause us to become mindless robots, endlessly repeating scriptures, or to become people who glibly attempt to order God around. Nor is the speaking of God's Word supposed to become a kind of Eastern mystical affirmation whereby reality is changed through the constant repetition of a word or idea. There is one particular Eastern cult that teaches chanting and repetition in order to bring about certain changes in a person's life. This is not what the Word of God is teaching. What the Book of Joshua and what Jesus Christ are teaching is the power and authority that is released when we speak God's Word with wisdom and grace. Like all great truths, it can be perverted and distorted. But the fact remains that speaking God's Word properly allows for the extension of His kingdom rule in our lives.

The Book of Joshua also talks about meditating on God's Word. Unlike Eastern meditation, which encourages emptying of the mind and a general passivity, when the Bible speaks about meditating on the Word of God, it means constantly thinking about a particular passage of Scripture and gleaning all the great truths it contains. This may involve opening a Bible, reading a particular verse or passage over and over again, and asking God to reveal its meaning to you. It may involve shutting out all other thoughts except for a Bible verse and shutting ourselves up before God so that we can hear His voice.

Finally, the power of God's Word is fully released in our lives when we obey and do what the Word of God says. Deuteronomy 28:1 says, "Now it shall come to pass, if you diligently obey the voice of the LORD your God, to observe carefully all His commandments which I command you today, that the LORD your God will set you high above all nations of the earth." What a fantastic promise to those who do and obey the Word!

In James 1:22 this theme is repeated, "But be <u>doers of the word</u>, and not hearers only, deceiving yourselves." The power of God's Word is released and activated through faith and obedience.

    FAITH ALIVE

The power of God's Word can be released in our lives. However, we must actively meditate upon what His Word says so that this power can be released.

Power Principle:

"So then faith *comes* by hearing, and hearing by the word of God" (Rom. 10:17).

We can build our faith through reading, hearing, and meditating on the Word of God. Faith that is produced by hearing the Word of God will release God's power in our lives. If we would actively meditate on God's Word, we would avoid many of the problems of life. In Psalm 119:92, we read: "Unless Your law *had been* my delight, I would then have perished in my affliction."

Exercise:

Ask yourself, "What afflictions am I perishing from in my life?"

a. spiritual

b. financial

c. physical

d. other

How can you release the power of God's Word into that area of your life through delighting in the Word and meditating in it?

1. From *Evangelizing the New Age* © 1989 by Paul McGuire. Published by Servant Publications, P.O. Box 8617, Ann Arbor, Michigan 48107. Used with Permission.

2. *Spirit-Filled Life Bible* (Nashville, TN: Thomas Nelson Publishers, 1991), 1876, "Word Wealth: 4:12 powerful."

3. Ibid., 1665, "Word Wealth: 19:20 word."

4. Ibid., 1876, "Kingdom Dynamics: Understanding *Rhema* and *Logos*."

5. Ibid., 1408, "Word Wealth: 4:4 word."

Lesson 7/ The Power of the Blood for the Individual, Family, and Nation

The blood of Jesus is powerful. It protects, as in the case of the Passover blood protecting the children of Israel in Egypt. It purges away sin, as in the case of Jesus, the Lamb of God, taking away the sins of the world. And it pulverizes Satan, our enemy, in his attempts to neutralize our testimony to the truth of God's Word in our lives.

THE PASSOVER LAMB

In Exodus 12:1–7, 12, 13 (read these verses), the Lord spoke to Moses about executing judgment against the gods of Egypt. He told Moses to tell the people of Israel to place the blood of a lamb on the doorposts of their homes as a means of supernatural protection in what has come to be known as the Passover.

From these verses we learn that God was going to judge supernaturally the gods of Egypt. In this final visitation, God showed that He was greater than the Egyptian god Osiris, the Egyptian giver of life. However, through the blood of the covenant God would deliver Israel from death. All Israel had to do was apply the blood of a lamb on the doorposts of their homes in what came to be known as the Passover. In addition, they were commanded by God to have a Passover meal consisting of roasted lamb, bitter herbs and unleavened bread.

In our day, God's judgment is once again upon the land, not in the sense of God's specifically sending death upon the firstborn, but when a nation, culture, or home walks away from the life-giving principles that God established to worship the false gods of pleasure, self, and materialism; when a people deliberately choose to walk away from the truths that God established, they also walk away from God's protective covering. Thus death, disease, and destruction are loosed. This doesn't happen because God is sitting up in heaven waiting to hurl thunderbolts of judgment upon them. But just as a man or a woman, throwing aside his or her umbrella in a rainstorm, is going to get wet, so are those who forsake God's protective covering. They are prey to natural and supernatural forces that bring destruction.

Divorce, child abuse, AIDS, poverty, drug addiction, alcoholism, sexual problems, disease, and occult forces seek to ravage the home in our time in order to destroy it. It is precisely here in the nitty-gritty of life that the blood of the covenant has the supernatural power to stop these forces in our homes and nation. Once again, the blood of the covenant or blood of the Lamb has the power to render evil inoperative in our families and nation. Just as the ancient Hebrews applied the blood of a lamb on the doorposts of their homes, so in our day we can apply the blood of the Lamb—Jesus Christ—on the doorposts of our homes!

What this means is that as we choose to walk under the covering of the blood in our homes, we can appropriate the supernatural power of blood to break the power of Satan in our homes. On a practical level, the blood of the Lamb breaks the generational curse over families and destroys the bondages of alcoholism, drug addiction, sexual problems, disease, death, and occult forces that have been passed down from our ancestors. The blood of the Lamb is a living supernatural property that can cleanse us from the most deep-rooted bondages of sin and despair. It has literal wonder-working power to cleanse us from the decay and erosion that sin brings, and it bathes us in the pure rejuvenating flow of the Spirit of God. The blood of Jesus Christ binds up the shame and releases us to experience the fullness of His glory—the awesome wonder, majesty, and glory of the Lamb upon the throne, the triumphant Christ who brings us before the very throne room of God as children of His heavenly family, to live forever with Him in the splendor of eternity!

Keeping in mind the dynamic truths recorded in Exodus 12:1–7, 12, 13, how can we practically apply the blood of the covenant to our lives today? Answer the following questions to help appropriate the blood of the Lamb, Jesus Christ, to your daily life.

How can I apply the blood over the doorposts of my home? (Ex. 12:7)

How does the blood keep away evil from my dwelling? (Ex. 12:13)

How can I appropriate the power of the blood over the lives of my loved ones? (Acts 16:31)

How can I appropriate the power of the blood over the community, city, and nation where I live? (2 Chr. 7:14)

JESUS CHRIST IS THE LAMB OF GOD WHO TAKES AWAY THE SIN OF THE WORLD

John 1:29 says, "The next day John saw Jesus coming toward him, and said, 'Behold! The Lamb of God who takes away the sin of the world!'" Jesus Christ is the very embodiment of the blood of the covenant as the Lamb of God. It is He alone who has the power to remove man's sin through His sacrificial death. Through the blood of the Lamb of God the power of sin over our lives is broken and Satan no longer has a foothold in us. When we lived in spiritual darkness we lived under the rulership of the god of this age. However, when we received Jesus Christ into our lives by faith, we died with Christ and are no longer bound to sin and this satanic age. In the cosmic courts of heaven we have been set free by the power of the blood. The blood of God is so powerful it delivers us from the kingdom of darkness and satanic rule (Col. 1:13). We are no longer slaves to sin because of the blood. Jesus Christ is the Lamb of God whose precious life blood has set us free from sin's power.

    ### WORD WEALTH

Sin, *hamartia.* Literally, "missing the mark," failure, offense, taking the wrong course, wrongdoing, sin, guilt. The New Testament uses the word in a generic sense for concrete wrongdoing.[1]

The blood of the Lamb of God supernaturally releases us from the dominion and power of Satan's grasp. It has within it enough power to change the course of human history forever. We must learn to think of the blood as more than a red liquid within the body. When it comes to the blood of Christ, there is an actual supernatural property within it that has a power so great that it can transform the very universe. The property of the blood of the Lamb can take people who are in the grips of spiritual and physical death and bring them into eternity. Praise God!

In answering these questions, we will see how the supernatural power of the blood can transform lives:

How can the power of the blood take away my sin? (Heb. 9:14)

How can the power of the blood completely transform my life?

How is Jesus Christ the Lamb of God? (John 1:29)

How does Jesus Christ's being the Lamb of God relate to the blood of the covenant? (Heb. 9:12)

THE POWER OF THE BLOOD CAN EFFECTIVELY BREAK SATAN'S ATTEMPT AT DOMINION IN OUR LIVES

All of us live in a world that is contaminated by the death force of sin. This contamination puts us under the dominion of the god of this age. The power to resist temptation is dismantled. In other words, nonbelievers find themselves moving according to the world spirit of this present age. It is for this reason that the world continues to move in a direction that is evil. It is a natural thing to do because it is going with the flow of this world system.

When confronting the world spirit of this age we need to ask ourselves the question, "How can the death force of sin and the very real forces of evil be destroyed by the power of the blood?" (Eph. 1:7)

Keeping in mind that Christ's blood is far more than just a red liquid that coursed through His veins, describe how the blood of Jesus Christ is a supernatural property that contains the power of God to dismiss darkness forever and bring people into the fullness of the light. (Acts 26:18)

How are the powers of darkness and the grip of Satan broken as the rejuvenating stream of God's life force (eternal life) is released through the blood? (Rev. 12:11)

How are the bondages and grips of hell's fury removed as the presence of God within the blood is released? (Heb. 9:14)

To repeat, it is important to deepen our understanding of Christ's blood as far more than the red liquid that coursed through His veins. The blood of Jesus Christ is a real and supernatural property that contains the power of God to dismiss the darkness forever and bring people into the fullness of the light. The blood of Jesus Christ is a supernatural property that possesses the life force of God Himself. Therefore when this blood was shed for the sins of humankind, the enormous power of God's life force within it was released. Eternal life was activated. Subsequently, the grip of Satan and the powers of darkness are broken as the rejuvenating stream of God's life force is introduced into the human personality. In other words, the bondages and grips of hell's fury are removed as the presence of God within the blood of the Lamb is released.

When the phrase *power in the blood* is used, it is referring to the supernatural power that is contained in Christ's blood. This power is able to banish Satan, sin, and darkness with the very force of its holy presence. The consuming fire of God's holiness purges darkness and the dominion of sin with a force often not recognized in religious circles.

What the power of the blood means in the most real terms is that the power of Jesus Christ is readily available to anyone who needs it! Thus, when hell's forces are arrayed against us and the fury of demonic forces is at the very worst, the blood makes it possible for us to find salvation, healing, and deliverance. As the blood of the Lamb flows from Calvary into our lives, marriages are restored, victims of abuse are healed, bodies are freed from disease, occult energy is banished, oppression is lifted and the invading army of God's incredible glory is released into our lives at every dimension.

In prayer, it is common to *plead the blood*. Although there is no direct reference to this phrase in the Bible, it is clear that the blood of Jesus Christ—the blood of the Lamb—has great power in our lives. In Revelation 12:11 the scripture reads, "And they overcame him by the blood of the Lamb and by the word of their testimony." *Pleading the blood*—applying the power of the blood of Jesus Christ—is simply making use of this divine resource that God has given us. When we apply the blood of Jesus Christ in our lives we are making use of this divine resource by faith.

FAITH ALIVE

How can we, as individuals, apply the power of the blood over our homes? What specific steps must we take to appropriate the blood's power, or *plead the blood,* over our lives? The following is a suggested prayer exercise in appropriating this power:

Go to God in prayer and appropriate the power of the blood over your home and family. Begin by spending some time in worship and praise before Him. Allow His presence to fill you and His glory to be poured out in your midst.

As a priest and intercessor for your family, your prayer might be something like this: *"Father, in the name of Jesus, I come to You and worship You. I praise Your name, Jesus! God, I come to You, cleansed in the blood of the Lamb. I plead that blood [or, apply the blood] over my home and family. I bind the powers of darkness. In Jesus' name, amen."*

1. *Spirit-Filled Life Bible* (Nashville, TN: Thomas Nelson Publishers, 1991), 1575, "Word Wealth: 1:29 sin."

Lesson 8/Entering God's Presence Through the Blood

It is not possible to live without sin in this life (1 John 1:8), but it is possible to live with a clear conscience (Acts 24:16). How does this work?

GOING BOLDLY TO THE THRONE OF GRACE

Hebrews 4:16 tells us that we can go boldly to the throne of grace. "Let us therefore come boldly to the throne of grace, that we may obtain mercy and find grace to help in time of need." The gospel of Jesus Christ is called the Good News because through the blood of Jesus Christ we can be cleansed of our sins, shortcomings, mistakes, and failures. This is liberating, because it means that anyone can come to God if they ask for forgiveness. The key concept here is the word *grace.*

 WORD WEALTH

Grace, *charis.* From the same root as *chara,* "joy," and *chairo,* "to rejoice." *Charis* causes rejoicing. It is the word for God's grace as extended to sinful man. It signifies unmerited favor, undeserved blessing, free gift.[1]

The Bible teaches us that salvation is a free gift from God. In addition, we are encouraged to "come boldly to the throne of grace" regularly in our Christian walk. The reason this is good news is because of the blood of Jesus Christ. We can be confident that when we go to God we will receive unmerited favor and undeserved blessing. In other words, God does not treat us on the basis of how good we have been during the week or how spiritual. His love and goodness toward us is constant because of grace.

After studying the word *grace*, write in your own words how salvation is a free gift from God. (Eph. 2:8)

Second, how does understanding that salvation is a free gift based on unmerited favor apply to Hebrews 4:16? In other words, why can I go boldly to the throne of grace?

In our society, we hear the phrase *unconditional love* used constantly. The reason for this is that our society does not practice unconditional love. Instead, human love is dispensed on the basis of how well you measure up or perform. Thus, love is conditional. The result of this is that people are placed in a psychological bondage and never feel quite good enough or measure up.

When it comes to ideas about God, people generally feel unworthy and that they do not measure up. They attempt to alleviate this feeling through doing good things or trying to be spiritual. Yet this is exactly the opposite of what the Bible teaches. Ephesians 2:8, 9 states: "For by grace you have been saved through faith, and that not of yourselves; *it is* the gift of God, not of works, lest anyone should boast." The idea here is that it is impossible to earn acceptance with God. It's not that good works are bad. It's simply that no amount of good works can make a person holy or pure enough to be justified in God's sight. Trying to please God with good works is the spiritual equivalent of trying to fill an ocean with a teaspoon of water. The whole notion is rather preposterous. Yet, in a spiritual sense, this is exactly what every other religion teaches.

After reading Ephesians 2:8, 9, write down in your own words the answer to the question, "Why is it impossible to earn acceptance with God?"

People have an innate desire to be unconditionally loved. However, in the area of human relationships, they have no real basis for finding unconditional love. And in relationship to a holy God, men and women are truly sinners, and this reality cannot just be swept under the carpet. Fortunately, God has provided a way for us to be totally accepted and loved by God. It is through the blood of Jesus Christ that God does away with sin. Since the sin is removed by the blood, man can come to God as a holy and pure being, justified by grace. This truth is revealed in Romans 3:24: "Being justified freely by His grace through the redemption that is in Christ Jesus."

What reason does the above verse give us for God's unconditional love?

Therefore, God is free to love us *unconditionally* only after the *condition* of sin has been removed through the blood. The same principle follows through in human relationships. Only people who have experienced being loved by God and who have the love of God in them through the Holy Spirit can truly love others. First John 4:7, 8 states: "Beloved, let us love one another, for love is of God; and everyone who loves is born of God and knows God. He who does not love does not know God, for God is love."

Why is it that only people who love God and know God's love personally can truly love unconditionally? (1 John 4:7, 8)

 WORD WEALTH

Love, *agape.* A word to which Christianity gave new meaning. *Agape* denotes an undefeatable benevolence and unconquerable goodwill that always seeks the highest good of the other person, no matter what he does. It is the self-giving love that gives freely without asking anything in return, and does not consider the worth of its object. *Agape* describes the unconditional love God has for the world.[2]

The key truth here is that *God is love.* You cannot remove God from the equation of love and still have love. When the world talks about unconditional love, they always come up empty because they have removed God, who is love, out of the equation.

The following explores the concepts of grace, love, and the blood of Jesus Christ:

Why does grace give me the confidence to go to God in prayer? (1 John 5:14)

How does the blood of Christ make it possible for me to go to the throne of grace? (Heb. 4:16)

Why can I really love others only after I have known the love of God? (1 John 4:7, 8)

What does *agape* love mean? How is it different from other kinds of love? (Rom. 5:8; 1 John 4:10)

THE BLOOD OF CHRIST CLEANSES US FROM ALL SIN

In 1 John 1:7–10 we read about the provision God has made for us if we sin.

The international ministry of Campus Crusade for Christ teaches a principle called spiritual breathing. The idea is that a Christian regularly confesses to God his or her sins in prayer and asks God to cleanse him or her. Confession is as natural as exhaling. The goal is to stay spiritually alive by not allowing any unconfessed sin to remain in our lives.

Why do all of us in our daily lives miss the mark of God's standard of holiness and why do we need to regularly ask God for forgiveness? (1 John 1:9)

How does this relate to Campus Crusade's teaching of spiritual breathing and 1 John 1:7–10?

Take a moment and pray, asking God to show you areas where you have missed the mark and sinned. Perhaps you made an unkind remark to somebody or gave in to a deliberate indulgence of something you knew to be wrong. Also, wrong attitudes, unforgiveness, and lovelessness all fall into the category of sin. How can you apply the principle of spiritual breathing to these areas? (1 John 1:9)

 WORD WEALTH

Sin, *hamartia.* Literally, "missing the mark," failure, offense, taking the wrong course, wrongdoing, sin, guilt.[3]

In our humanistic society, sin is often dealt with by saying that sin no longer exists. Along with this denial, an entirely new vocabulary is created in order to justify sin or rationalize it out of existence. For example, a person who commits adultery is having an *affair,* and homosexuality is called being *gay.* Below, list three other words that fall into this category, and then write down the word or phrase each replaced.

1.

2.

3.

Yet, despite all the word games, depression is at an all-time high in our culture. Some philosophers have called this the *Age of Anxiety.* The reason for this is that God created humankind as moral beings. When we violate God's laws, we innately feel guilty. Consciences may be hardened and people may appear to not feel any guilt. However, the prevalence of depression, suicide and anxiety and the widespread use of tranquilizers, drugs, and alcohol, suggest that people are not as immune from violating God's laws as they think.

Fortunately, God has given us a path to total freedom and a means of doing away with guilt and sin through the blood of Jesus. If we confess our sins to God, we can be set free from the prisons of anxiety, depression, and guilt. However, in order to apply these principles, we must have a firm grasp of what they mean in our life. The following prayer exercise can help us more fully understand the reality of Christ's forgiveness in our lives:

PRACTICAL PRAYER EXERCISE

Based on 1 John 1:9, spend a few moments and go to God in prayer and ask Him to search your heart and reveal any sin in your life that needs to be confessed. Begin by praising and worshiping Him. Enter His presence with thanksgiving!

Second, ask God to search your heart with His Holy Spirit and reveal to you anything that is displeasing to Him. Do not be afraid to listen. He is not here to condemn you, but to help you grow.

Listen to Him as He reveals shortcomings to you, and then ask to be forgiven for these. Ask His help and grace in following His will.

Finally, praise and thank Him for His forgiveness. Spend some time worshiping Him. Allow yourself to experience a release in your spirit through the cleansing of the blood.

Once you have brought any sin under the blood, you should not allow yourself to feel any condemnation. Being cleansed by the blood should be a life-changing and refreshing experience!

CONFIDENCE THROUGH OVERCOMING CONDEMNATION

Psychologists recognize that the suppression of unresolved guilt can bring about severe psychological problems. Unforgiveness, resentment, hurt, and woundedness all gnaw at the inner personality. The blood of Jesus Christ brings forgiveness and healing. However, even after forgiveness has been asked of God, many people still live under a dark cloud of condemnation and guilt. In the book *A Man's Confidence—A Study of How Men Can Become Confident in Life Through Mastering Guilt*, Jack Hayford relates how to overcome guilt and condemnation as God revealed the truth to him from 1 John 1:9: "If we confess our sins, He is faithful and just to forgive us our sins and to cleanse us from all unrighteousness."

Dr. Hayford outlines the crippling effects that condemnation can produce in our lives:

1. Condemnation shakes our assurance toward God. Shaken assurance is a kind of spiritual and emotional drain-off that deadens the soul's sensitivities.

2. Condemnation cripples our confidence in daily living.

3. Condemnation evaporates our certainty for ministry. This crippling effect of condemnation pinches off God's life flow through us.

Dr. Hayford suggests that the solution to the problem of condemnation is the truth of God's mighty Word (Ps. 36:9). "The entrance of Your words gives light; it gives understanding to the simple" (Ps. 119:30). It is the light of God's Word that tells us, "He is faithful and just to forgive us *our* sins, and to cleanse us from all unrighteousness" (1 John 1:9).

It has been said that the Holy Spirit convicts us of sin (John 16:8), but Satan condemns us.

In Revelation 12:10 Satan is called "the accuser of our brethren." "Then I heard a loud voice saying in heaven, 'Now salvation, and strength, and the kingdom of our God, and the power of His Christ have come, for the accuser of our brethren, who accused them before our God day and night, has been cast down.'" Here we see that Satan is busy accusing Christians before the throne room of God.

What we must understand is that the Devil is a liar and the Father of lies. In John 8:44 Jesus Christ said, "You are of *your* father the devil, and the desires of your father you want to do. He was a murderer from the beginning, and *does not* stand in the truth, because there is no truth in him. When he speaks a lie, he speaks from his own *resources,* for he is a liar and the father of it."

Satan, or the Father of lies, accuses us before the throne room of God. In addition, the spirit of the Devil works through other people and even friends to attempt to undermine the believer with subtle accusations about their motives and character. The purpose of this Satanic propaganda campaign is to destroy our effectiveness for Jesus Christ.

Yet, like all liars, Satan uses grains of truth. There may be things about our personality or behavior that God has not perfected yet. However, we are under grace and not the Law. We have been cleansed by the blood of the Lamb. Our righteousness is not in and of ourselves, but our righteousness is in Christ. God views us as totally sinless and pure through the blood of Jesus Christ. Therefore, as we grow as believers, we never have to feel condemned or accused, because the blood of Jesus Christ cleanses us from all sin.

Thus, when Satan or our conscience or people attempt to accuse us, undermine us, and use subtle remarks to get at us, we do not have to feel guilty and condemned, because our sins and failures are under the blood! As we endeavor to live for Christ, the Devil and people will seek to remind us of our shortcomings. However, because of the blood, we are set free from those accusations. This doesn't mean that we may not need to grow, change, or mature. But, in the process of being perfected, we are free to enjoy our relationship with God.

The Devil, or the serpent of old, is crafty and a trickster. He will deliberately attempt to set up traps in our lives so that we will fail and miss God's mark. Then he will be there to condemn and accuse us. Satan's game plan is to destroy our effectiveness for Jesus Christ through accusation and condemnation. But when we understand what the blood of Jesus Christ does for us, we never have to be victimized by this dark strategy again.

However, there may be places in our lives where repentance and confession of sin are necessary. We may have to choose to turn away from sin and walk the paths of righteousness. As believers in Jesus Christ, we cannot be forced by the Devil to do anything. God has given us a free will and the power to choose what is right. Every believer in Jesus Christ will experience conflict in their souls as they walk with Jesus Christ. The apostle Paul explained it this way: "For the good that I will to do, I do not do; but the evil I will not to do, that I practice" (Rom. 7:19). Paul analyzed the spiritual conflict inside each believer and recognized that the sin nature inside of us has to be put to death by faith in the power of Christ. The apostle Paul declared in Romans 8:1, *"There* is therefore now no condemnation to those who are in Christ Jesus, who do not walk according to the flesh, but according to the Spirit."

 FAITH ALIVE

<u>Unmasking the Satanic Traps</u>

It is vitally important that, as believers in Jesus Christ, we recognize the traps and strategies that Satan will attempt to use against us. In Ephesians 6:11 we are admonished: "Put on the whole armor of God, that you may be able to stand against the wiles of the Devil." In Genesis 3:1 we read, "Now the serpent was more cunning than any beast of the field which the LORD God had made."

We must recognize that condemnation and accusation are two of the Devil's prime strategies in attempting to destroy our effectiveness in Jesus Christ.

Furthermore, we must understand that there are patterns that he uses. Once we recognize the satanic game plan, then we can learn to apply the blood of Jesus Christ more effectively.

After prayerful consideration, list and identify areas in which you have been tempted to sin and feel condemned in a kind of vicious cycle or treadmill experience.

For example, whenever circumstances pile up in your life and you are under pressure, you may find that you lose your temper and say things that you shouldn't. Then immediately afterward, you feel condemned and unworthy. The Devil comes to you and tells you that you are a terrible witness for Jesus Christ. How can God use you?

The solution is for you to recognize that you are still growing in grace. Although you did lose your temper, you have already confessed it to God. It is under the blood. Therefore, you are free from condemnation!

Use the list below to unmask these satanic traps and treadmill experiences.

1. Write down the area in which you have sinned. For example: Whenever pressure comes into my life and I am tired, I seem to lose my temper and say things that I shouldn't.

2. Identify the cycle of condemnation and the satanic trap. For example: After I have lost my temper, I feel condemned and unworthy before God. I feel that I am not a good example of a Christian and that God will not use me.

3. Recognize the power of the blood to set you free! Write down how that power has set you free from condemnation (Rom. 8:1). For example: I have confessed my sin of losing my temper, and God has forgiven me. I am growing in grace and asking God to mature me so that when pressure comes, I will have victory over my temper. Until that time, I am free from condemnation. Because of the blood of Christ, God sees me as pure and holy. I am in Christ. There is no condemnation to those who are in Christ Jesus! Because of the blood of Christ, I am worthy and can be used by God. My righteousness is not of myself anyway. My righteousness is in Christ. I am free to walk in victory and worship the Lord, even after I stumble.

1. *Spirit-Filled Life Bible* (Nashville, TN: Thomas Nelson Publishers, 1991), 1766, "Word Wealth: 12:9 grace."

2. Ibid., 1694, "Word Wealth: 5:5 love."

3. Ibid., 1575, "Word Wealth: 1:29 sin."

Lesson 9/God's Word Is a Seed of Promised Fruit

Jesus said that His Father is glorified in His disciples' bearing much fruit (John 15:8). He said that this will happen "if you abide in Me, and My words abide in you" (John 15:7).

Keep planting the Word of God in your life. Abide in it (1) through staying close to Jesus and following Him and (2) through feeding on His Word and living it. Watch what happens. A fruitful harvest is coming your way (2 Cor. 9:6).

THE MILK AND MEAT OF THE WORD

In 1 Peter 2:2 we read that to grow spiritually as newborn Christians, we are supposed to regularly feed on the Word of God. Any parent knows that newborn babies drink a lot of milk. If they don't get milk then they begin to cry a lot! Little babies require regular feedings every three or four hours. They wiggle and squirm almost violently when they come near the mother's breast or a bottle until they begin to get the milk into their system.

This is precisely the analogy that God is using in the scripture. Newborn babies in Christ must have regular feedings of the Word of God if they are going to grow and stay alive spiritually. When people mature in Christ, they must have the meat of the Word or solid food. Hebrews 5:12, 14 illustrates this principle. The apostle Paul admonishes believers for their spiritual immaturity because they should have grown to the point where they need the solid food or meat of the Word. Instead, like little infants, they are still on milk.

What is the difference between the milk of the Word and solid food? (Heb. 5:12)

According to Hebrews 5:14, how do we know that we are ready for solid food?

For evidence of spiritual immaturity and the need for milk rather than solid food, read 1 Corinthians 3:1–3. In this passage we see the reference to spiritual immaturity and the need for the milk of the Word rather than the solid food of the Word. The apostle Paul states that envy, strife, and divisions are evidence of spiritual immaturity and carnality. Tragically, when we see the body of Christ today, we see a great deal of spiritual immaturity evidenced by envy, strife, and divisions. This is because many Christians are babes in Christ who are still feeding on the milk of the Word and not on solid food. They are behaving like mere men and not the children of God. When we eat of the solid food of the Word, we are transformed because our identity is changed. We begin to see ourselves in Christ, and our eternal destiny is unfolded.

What does it mean to behave like mere men? (1 Cor. 3:3)

What is the evidence of being a carnal Christian? (1 Cor. 3:1, 3)

THE SEED OF GOD'S WORD CAN PRODUCE PURPOSE, POWER, AND DESTINY

The great problem of today is that people have no vision or purpose. Proverbs 29:18 says, "Where *there is* no revelation, the people cast off restraint." Yet, through the Word of God, God promises to restore vision by the power of His outpoured Spirit. In Joel 2:28 the promise is made that "your young men shall see visions."

Keeping the truth of Joel 2:28 in mind, how does eating the solid food of God's Word on a daily basis restore vision and give purpose for our lives?

Why does reading the Word of God tell us who we are in Christ? (Rom. 8:16; 1 Pet. 1:23)

How can the regular reading of God's Word keep us from living as carnal or mere men? (1 Cor. 3:3; Eph. 5:26)

How does the Word of God have the power to transform our lives and regenerate us supernaturally? (James 1:18, 21)

Finally, why does the Adversary want to stop us from reading the Word of God? (Mark 4:15; John 10:10)

If we are living in what the Bible calls the last days, then God has a specific plan for this next generation. The thief (Satan) wants to steal, kill, and destroy that purpose. In order to do this, he attempts to block the seed of God's Word from finding its way into the hearts and minds of people, so that it cannot take root, grow, and bear fruit.

It is the entrance of God's Word into the human heart that brings undreamed fulfillment, purpose, and destiny. Is it any wonder that the forces of hell have an all-out strategy in blocking God's Word from the lives of people? Read Mark 4:13–20 for an outline of this principle of the seed of God's Word, which goes into human hearts and produces results if we allow it to. As you search your memory for people you have known who have accepted Jesus Christ or who have heard the Word of God, this parable becomes very real. We all know people who have been exposed to the Word of God but for whom "the cares of this world" and "the deceitfulness of riches" have choked the Word in their lives. They do not bear fruit.

Also, we know of people who have been exposed to an evangelistic message, but Satan takes away the Word that was sown in their hearts. Literally millions of people in our nation have heard the message of salvation by faith in Christ. However, Satan has stolen the Word from their hearts and they continue to walk in spiritual darkness. In 2 Corinthians 4:3, 4 we read how this happens. Millions in our nation and around the world who have heard the gospel of Jesus Christ have been blinded by "the god of this age." In fact, our entire culture (media and communications) is largely built on a foundation of spiritual deception. It has become a world information grid that, for the most part, attempts to lock out a biblical perspective and the reality of Jesus Christ.

Yet the brilliant truth of God's Word still pierces through the darkness, like stars that light up the night sky, declaring the glory and majesty of God in the midst of a dark age. John 1:5 states, "And the light shines in the darkness, and the darkness did not comprehend [overcome] it."

 WORD WEALTH

Comprehend, *katalambano*. The word is capable of three interpretations: 1) To seize, lay hold of, overcome. As such, John 1:5 could read, "The darkness does not gain control of it." 2) To perceive, attain, lay hold of with the mind; to apprehend with mental or moral effort. With this meaning the verse could be translated, "The darkness is unreceptive and does not understand it." 3) To quench, extinguish, snuff out the light by stifling it. "The darkness will never be able to eliminate it." Light and darkness essentially are antagonistic. The Christian's joy is in knowing that light is not only greater than darkness but will also outlast the darkness.[1]

Based on the above truth, why can we be confident that the Word of God will always overcome the darkness? (John 1:5)

What evidence do we have from Scripture that this is so? (1 John 2:8; Rev. 1:18)

WORD WEALTH

> **Darkness,** *scotia.* Darkness, gloom, evil, sin, obscurity, night, ignorance, moral depravity. The New Testament especially uses the word in the metaphorical sense of ignorance of divine truth, man's sinful nature, total absence of light, and a lack of spiritual perception. Light equals happiness. *Scotia* equals unhappiness. *Scotia* as spiritual darkness describes everything earthly or demonic that is at enmity with God.[2]

It is important that we grasp the importance of God's Word as a seed that is sown in men's hearts which has the capacity to change lives. The following questions will help us to understand that truth better.

How does Satan attempt to block the fruitfulness of the Word of God in people's lives? (Mark 4:18, 19)

When someone has the Word of God sown in their hearts, what does Satan try to do? (Mark 4:15)

On a personal level, how can we be sure that the Word of God, which has been sown into our hearts, is on good ground, and that we accept it and bear fruit thirty, sixty, and a hundred-fold? (2 Cor. 9:6; Gal. 6:9)

Satan is called "the god of this age." What is his role in blinding people from the truth in God's Word? (2 Cor. 4:3, 4)

How does the reality of John 1:5 give us confidence as we endeavor to be people who live the truth of the Word in a dark age?

How God's Word Refines and Purifies Us

The power of God's Word is like a seed that is able to refine, purify and change us into God's own image. It will take deep root in our souls and transform us from within. In James 1:21, we read that the implanted Word is able to save our souls. What precisely does this word "souls" actually mean? How can the implanted Word change our lives?

WORD WEALTH

Souls, *psuche.* Compare "psychology," "psychosis," "psychiatrist," "psychedelic." *Psuche* is the soul distinguished from the body. It is the seat of affections, will, desire, emotions, mind, reason, and understanding. *Psuche* is the inner self or the essence of life.[3]

When the Bible states that the implanted Word can save our souls, it means that the power of God's Word can change us as people. The Word of God can penetrate the depths of our will, desire, emotions, reason, and memory. The Word transforms us into what Christ wants us to be. The implanted Word can bring the healing power of God's Word into the very center of our being and set us free at the deepest dimensions. In practical terms, the implanted Word can do what no drug, psychotherapeutic technique or human self-help system can do. The implanted Word can enter us at the depths of our humanity and deliver us from fear, insecurity, addictions, bondage, oppression, and any form of darkness. The implanted Word can literally rescue us from life's prisons and bring us into the kingdom of light and joy for all eternity. Once again, the darkness cannot overcome the light. Therefore, the implanted Word is the entrance of God's Word, bringing light to our inner person and setting the captive free! We are new men and women in Jesus Christ who have been brought out of the kingdom of darkness into the marvelous kingdom of God's light. It is the Word of God that has the power and force to accomplish this.

How do I receive the implanted Word into my soul? (James 1:21)

How does the implanted Word save my soul? (James 1:21)

In James 1:22–25 we read not only of hearing the Word of God but of doing the Word of God. Read this passage, and answer the following questions:

In practical terms, how can we be people who apply the truth of James 1:22–25 and be doers of the Word?

James 1:22–25 warns us of the danger of merely reading the Word and not acting upon it. What steps can we take as believers to insure that we really act upon what we hear?

In addition, when we look into "the perfect law of liberty," the light of God's Word purifies us and calls us to allow the implanted Word to conform us into the image of Jesus Christ. Looking into "the perfect law of liberty" and reading the Word of God is like looking into a supernatural mirror. It not only reveals to us who we really are, but it also has the power to re-create us into the image of the One in whose image we were originally made. The Word of God is unlike any earthly mirror.

It not only has the capacity of showing us what we look like spiritually, but it also contains the power to change our very image or reflection into the image of Christ.

How can we make sure that we are doers of the Word and not hearers only? (James 1:22)

What does it mean to look into the perfect law of liberty? (James 1:25)

 FAITH ALIVE

The Bible teaches us that it is important to be a doer of the Word and not just a hearer (James 1:22). After prayerful consideration, list below five areas in which you feel that you personally need to both hear and do what the Word of God says. Include references to Bible verses that support your feeling.

EXAMPLE:

Areas where I need to do what the Word says: **Scripture verse:**

1. I need to do what God says in the area of   Malachi 3:10
tithes. What should I do specifically to obey
God in this area and become a doer of the
Word of God?

Areas where I need to do what the Word says: **Scripture verse:**

1.

2.

3.

4.

5.

1. *Spirit-Filled Life Bible* (Nashville, TN: Thomas Nelson Publishers, 1991), 1573, "Word Wealth: 1:5 comprehend."

2. Ibid., 1599, "Word Wealth: 12:46 darkness."

3. Ibid., 1557, "Word Wealth: 21:19 souls."

Lesson 10/Partaking in the Blood of the Covenant

The disciples, after hearing Jesus say, "For My flesh is food indeed, and My blood is drink indeed" (John 6:55), were tempted to follow Jesus no more (John 6:66, 67). They called this "a hard saying" and were stumped by it. How about us? Let's press in to understand and to receive the blessing of our Lord Jesus' table.

THE BLOOD OF THE NEW COVENANT

In Luke 22:15–20 Jesus Christ instituted what is known as the Lord's Supper. This took place during the Passover, which commemorated the time when God had freed the Israelites from their bondage in Egypt. On the night before they were to be freed, God had instructed the Israelites to smear blood on the doorposts of their homes so that death would pass over their homes. In this supper with His disciples, Jesus Christ explained the power and purpose of the New Covenant. His blood would cause "spiritual death" to pass over the lives of His followers. Through His blood, they would gain eternal life. Take time to read this passage from Luke 22 now.

What Jesus Christ was explaining to His disciples was that the very fulfillment and final expression of the blood covenant was to be found in the New Covenant. On it, the blood of Jesus Christ was to be the atonement for our sins and the sins of the world. The blood of innocent animals in the Old Testament, beginning with the tunic God made for Adam and Eve and the Old Testament animal sacrifices, including the blood on the doorposts during the Passover, simply pointed the way to the blood of Jesus Christ. For it was through Christ's blood on the Cross that humankind would be redeemed from sin. The bondage of sin that Adam and Eve had unleashed upon the human race in the Garden of Eden because they had disobeyed the Word of God would be undone by the power of Christ's blood. When Jesus Christ said, "This cup *is* the new covenant in My blood, which is shed for you" (Luke 22:20), He was explaining that, through the shedding of His blood, they would experience release from their sins and freedom from their captivity to Satan's dominion.

The power of the blood, released in the New Covenant by the shedding of Christ's blood, broke the power of sin and death forever. The dominion that Satan gained, through Adam and Eve's disobedience to the Word, would be overturned by the power of the blood. The Lord's Supper, or communion, is not merely a religious ritual. It is communion in the literal sense of the word. We experience supernatural communion with the living God because of the blood of Jesus. There is an awesome power, wonder, and majesty that is released when we, as ordinary people, can be lifted into the presence of the Infinite One through the blood of Jesus Christ.

In answering the following questions, go back and read Genesis 3. Then from your own understanding, answer the question, How did Adam and Eve lose their communion with God through disobedience? (Gen. 3:8)

How did they attempt to regain this oneness and communion with God through their own self-effort? (Gen. 3:7)

Then look at Luke 22:15–20 in light of Genesis 3. How did this cup of the New Covenant speak to what happened in Genesis 3?

Why is it only through the blood of Jesus Christ or the blood of the New Covenant that this oneness or communion with God can be restored? (Luke 22:20)

Finally, after reading and understanding the spiritual dynamic that caused the Fall of Man in Genesis 3 and the *restoration* of man with God brought about by the cup of the New Covenant that Jesus Christ talked to His disciples about in Luke 22:15–20, answer this question: How is the same deception of the serpent that caused Adam and Eve to disobey God's Word in the Garden at work today in attempting to deceive people from the reality and power of what Jesus Christ talked about when He said, "This cup *is* the new covenant in My blood, which is shed for you"? (2 Cor. 4:4)

There is such confusion surrounding the gospel of Jesus Christ and the message of the blood of Christ because Satan understands that, if people ever understood the New Covenant of the blood of Jesus Christ and accepted it, they would be set free from his dominion. It is no accident that in our culture the message of the Cross is mocked and ridiculed. Ministers who have fallen are paraded constantly in the mass media. The demons of hell have a vested interest in blinding people to the truth and reality of the gospel of Jesus Christ. A gospel that is based on the death and resurrection of Jesus Christ and His shed blood is greater than the sins of any man or woman alive, including those who have fallen in public disgrace. The blood of Jesus Christ has destroyed the power of sin, death, and the authority of Satan over humankind. The blood of Jesus Christ is the most powerful force on this earth. The blood of Jesus Christ is the Word of God energized and active in redeeming humankind from the mistake that Adam and Eve passed on through the generations. It literally removes the power of sin or the death force and infuses individuals with God's very eternal nature, once again. The blood of Jesus Christ acts like a heavenly transfusion, where the contaminated blood, infected with the death force, is removed. The very life of God Himself is reintroduced into the human system through the blood of Jesus Christ.

The ramifications of the blood of Jesus Christ's being transfused into humankind through the Cross of Christ is a complete reworking of what happened in Eden. Adam, Eve, and their children are no longer naked before God. Those who have accepted Jesus Christ into their lives are covered and walk in supernatural fellowship or communion with their Heavenly Father. Through the blood of Jesus Christ a doorway is created for each of us to enter the kingdom of God and live with God eternally, both now and forever, in heaven.

Is it any wonder that the "serpent of old" has mobilized all of hell's forces in attempting to keep humankind from this truth? The power of the blood brings about complete restoration between God and man that was lost through disobedience in Eden. This is precisely what Jesus Christ meant when He said, "This cup *is* the new covenant in My blood, which is shed for you."

Let us examine Christ's statement as recorded in Luke 22:20: "This cup *is* the new covenant in My blood, which is shed for you." The following questions will help us to examine this truth:

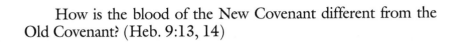

How is the blood of the New Covenant different from the Old Covenant? (Heb. 9:13, 14)

What is the similarity between the Passover celebration and the Lord's Supper? (Ex. 12:3–11; 1 Cor. 11:23–26)

How is the power of the blood celebrated in the Lord's Supper? (Matt. 26:28)

How is the power of Satan destroyed through the blood of the New Covenant? (Heb. 9:14; Rev. 12:11)

THE FULL SCOPE OF COMMUNION

In partaking of the blood of the New Covenant, it is important that we understand the full scope of communion in our lives.

Dr. Jack Hayford, in his powerful message entitled "The Full Scope of Communion," gives us five great principles of communion. These principles are outlined here:

1. Communion Is a Celebration of Victory

In Revelation 12:10, 11, we read:

> Then I heard a loud voice saying in heaven, "Now salvation, and strength, and the kingdom of our God, and the power of His Christ have come, for the accuser of our brethren, who accused them before our God day and night, has been cast down. And they overcame him by the blood of the Lamb and by the word of their testimony."

The first principle Dr. Hayford outlined was the reminder that communion is a celebration of the New Covenant. Christ won the victory over the Devil for us. Although many churches still take communion in a morose sense, the spirit of communion is a triumphant and victorious one, where we are to be reminded that Jesus Christ conquered the power of the enemy! Jesus Christ told us to drink of the cup of the blood of the New Covenant and to "do this in remembrance of Me." We are to remember that Jesus Christ is the Lamb of God whose blood redeemed us from the power of sin, death, and Satan.

The Lord's Supper—communion or "eucharist"—comes from the Greek word *eucharisteo*, which means to give thanks.

WORD WEALTH

Given thanks, *eucharisteo*. From *eu*, "well," and *charizomai*, "to give freely." To be grateful, to express gratitude, to be thankful. Eleven of the thirty-nine appearances of the word in the New Testament refer to partaking of the Lord's Supper, while twenty-eight occurrences describe praise words given to the Godhead. During the second century, Eucharist became the generic term for the Lord's Supper.[1]

The purpose of communion, or the Lord's Supper, is to "give thanks." Communion is to be a celebration of victory.

2. Communion Is a Proclamation of Redemption

First Corinthians 11:26 reads, "For as often as you eat this bread and drink this cup, you proclaim the Lord's death till He comes." When we take communion, we are to take it as a "proclamation of redemption." The only way God could redeem humankind was through the blood of Jesus Christ. Humankind was in need of a Redeemer and "redeeming costs something." Every time we come to the Lord's Table, we are saying, "Jesus died for us; Jesus is my victory, and a price was paid." When we come to the Lord's Supper, we are to be reminded of specific things that God has done for us through His redemption. Communion means a "sharing in common." Together, as the body of Christ, we share what Jesus Christ has done for us.

3. Communion Is a Declaration of Dependence

In John 6:53 Jesus said, "Most assuredly, I say to you, unless you eat of the flesh of the Son of Man and drink His blood, you have no life in you." When we take communion, we are declaring our total dependence upon Jesus Christ and His power. As we surrender to His lordship and depend upon Him for our strength, a dynamism of the Holy Spirit is released in us when we partake of His body and blood. The New Covenant releases supernatural energy into our lives through the blood of Jesus Christ.

4. Communion Is an Examination of Self

Although communion is not to be a morose ritual, it is a time when we are to search our own hearts in the presence of God and ask to be cleansed from our sins through the blood of Jesus Christ. In 1 Corinthians 11:28, 29, we read, "But let a man examine himself, and so let him eat of the bread and drink of the cup. For he who eats and drinks in an unworthy manner eats and drinks judgment to himself, not discerning the Lord's body."

This particular passage of scripture is often misunderstood and used as a means of condemnation. However, the purpose of this scripture is to teach us to become true disciples who accept the discipline that discipleship brings. Thus we examine ourselves in the light of the Holy Spirit, allowing God's Spirit to point out in our lives areas in which we are "missing the mark." It is here that we take advantage of the blessing that the New Covenant brings. It is the complete forgiveness of sins through the blood of Jesus Christ. We must realize that all of us will sin as we walk with Christ in this life. Wrong attitudes, living in fear instead of faith, anger, jealousy, and deliberate sins must all be confessed before the Lord, so that we can receive healing, cleansing, and deliverance. Wrong attitudes and sins, like fear, can bring bondage into our lives and can actually prevent the full release of God's possibilities in our lives.

In understanding that one of the principles the Bible teaches regarding communion is an examination of self, how can we be sure that we do not turn a healthy examination of self into a morose and self-depreciating ritual? (1 Cor. 11:28)

What is the purpose of self-examination? (1 Cor. 11:29)

In practical terms, what should be the spiritual result of allowing God to fill our inner beings more completely? Can we rightfully expect to experience greater joy and victory in this process? (Eph. 3:16–21)

The power of the blood is that Jesus Christ sets us free to be all that we are created to be. Self-examination, although momentarily difficult, should always lead to personal resurrection and a greater infilling of the Spirit of God.

5. Communion Is a Reception of Provision

To partake of the Lord's Supper in an unworthy manner means that we do not allow the full power and provision of this cup of the New Covenant to be manifest in our lives (1 Cor. 11:29–32). In other words, we limit the full worth of the price He paid for our complete healing and deliverance.

The purpose of the blood of the New Covenant is that Jesus Christ paid not only for our sins, but for the full provision for every need in our lives. To take the Lord's Supper in an unworthy manner is to limit, by our unbelief, the full provision of what God has done. The New Covenant was made available to us by the price of Christ's blood and His death on the Cross. It provides healing, financial provision, peace of mind, deliverance, freedom from fear, and spiritual power and purpose. When we take communion, we are to believe that Jesus Christ's blood made it possible for us to receive the full worth of God's unlimited provision in every area of our lives! The awesome reality of this total provision, made possible by the blood of the covenant, should revolutionize our understanding of how good God is and how this goodness can be manifest in every area of our life.

 FAITH ALIVE

In the exercise below, apply the power and reality of what Christ meant when He said, "Do this in remembrance of Me." Although communion is best taken with other believers in a corporate setting, its wonder and power can be released privately with the Lord. Simply take some bread and grape juice in the privacy of your home or office and go to God in prayer. Begin by praising

Him, worshiping Him, and thanking Him in a celebration of victory. Thank Him for all of the blessings in your life.

Go to God in a proclamation of redemption. Thank Him for His death upon the Cross. Declare your dependence upon God as you eat of the bread and drink the juice, which is the blood of the New Covenant poured out for you and your family.

Then examine yourself in light of the Holy Spirit and allow God to deal with your heart about specific issues. Below are some sample issues that can be brought before the Lord:

1. Wrong attitudes that need to be confessed. Example: lovelessness toward someone you know or work with.

2. Living in fear, instead of faith in God's provisions, in some area of your life.

3. Anger toward God, or some person, instead of faith, trust, and forgiveness.

4. Tolerating some specific sin or indulgence in your life.

5. Other issues in your life that the Lord brings to mind.

In each of these areas, receive the forgiveness and cleansing properties of the blood of the Lamb. Allow yourself to be cleansed, refreshed, and delivered by the blood of the New Covenant. Praise the Lord, and thank Him for His forgiveness.

Finally, receive the full provision of the Lord by faith. Go to God in prayer. Ask Him in full confidence, specifically, for your needs or the needs of others. The blood of the covenant releases God's full provisions for whatever you need. Below are some specific areas in which you can trust God, through His covenant, to meet your need:

1. The provision for forgiveness of sins.

2. The provision for physical, mental, or spiritual healing.

3. The provision for deliverance from habits that bind or situations that imprison.

4. The provision for freedom from fear or oppression.

In your time of prayer, with thanksgiving, remember how God has performed miracles of provision for you in the past. Build your confidence in what God is going to do for you, now and in the future, by recounting what He has done for you in the past.

Write down five specific areas in which God has miraculously provided for you or your family in the past. Specifically recall what God has done for you when, in the past, you asked and received. Rejoice and praise Him for those miracles. Allow the reminder of past provisions to strengthen your heart for present situations.

1.

2.

3.

4.

5.

1. *Spirit-Filled Life Bible* (Nashville, TN: Thomas Nelson Publishers, 1991), 1583, "Word Wealth: 6:11 given thanks."

Lesson 11/Power for Daily Living

Paul writes, "Giving thanks to the Father who has qualified us to be partakers of the <u>inheritance</u> of the saints in the light" (Col. 1:12). But what good is our *inheritance* if in ignorance we do not receive it? Instead, let us investigate the *legacy* of our living Lord to us who believe.

EXCEEDINGLY GREAT AND PRECIOUS PROMISES

In 2 Peter 1:3, 4, we read that God has given us "exceedingly great and precious promises." These promises enable us to overcome both the powers of darkness and natural forces that exist here in this fallen world.

Since God and His Word are one, and Jesus Christ is the Word become flesh, then it should follow that the promises of God are Jesus Himself delivering us from this present evil age. This present world is corrupt because of lust, not just sexual lust, but a general and pervasive desire that becomes idolatrous. God created things, including sex, for humankind to enjoy in their proper perspective. However, humankind worships money, power, fame, sex, possessions, careers, and the creation itself above God. Read 1 John 2:15–17 for illustrations of this principle.

In reading 1 John 2:15–17, how do things like career, money, power, position, material things, sex, and the like, take the place of God in our lives and become gods that we serve? (1 John 2:15)

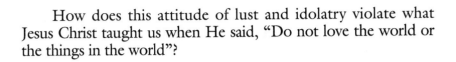

How does this attitude of lust and idolatry violate what Jesus Christ taught us when He said, "Do not love the world or the things in the world"?

How does the world encourage this attitude of lust?

In areas such as professional sports, business, and the entertainment industry, when does legitimate competition and the drive to excel cross over and become the "pride of life" and "the lust of the flesh"? (1 John 2:16)

At what point do legitimate interests and pursuits become idolatrous? How can we tell the difference? (Rom. 14:23)

Finally, how can we make sure that Jesus is really Lord of our lives and that we have not made idols out of other things? (1 John 2:6)

It is important that we understand how other things in our lives, even good things, can easily become idols or objects of worship. Below, list ten things that can easily become idols in our lives.

1._____

2._____

3._____

4._____

5._____

6._____

7._____

8._____

9._____

10._____

Even sex in our culture, through pornography, can become a god. Movie stars are sometimes called "sex symbols" or "sex goddesses."

When our pursuit of the things of this world becomes all-important—even to the point of breaking the commandments of God to get them—we fall into idolatry.

WORD WEALTH

Lusts, *epithuma.* A strong desire and intense craving for something. Three times it applies to good desires (Luke 22:15; Phil. 1:23; 1 Thess. 2:17). Its other uses are negative, such as gratifying sensual cravings, desiring the forbidden, longing for the evil, coveting what belongs to someone else, and striving for things, persons, or experiences contrary to the will of God.[1]

In the sexual area, sexual perversion, promiscuity, and homosexuality are the products of inordinate lusts. In Romans 1:25–27, the apostle Paul reveals that when men and women begin to worship sex rather than God, they are given up to vile passions. This is further emphasized in verses 28–32, from which we learn that such people lose the knowledge of God and are given over "to a debased mind." This fallen, or debased, mind produces people who are "filled with all unrighteousness, sexual immorality, wickedness, covetousness, maliciousness; full of envy, murder, strife, deceit, evil-mindedness; *they are* whisperers, back-biters, haters of God, violent, proud, boasters, inventors of evil things, disobedient to parents, undiscerning, untrustworthy, unloving, unforgiving, unmerciful."

What we see here is a perfect description of our modern culture, along with its dysfunctional families. The "trash television," scandal magazines, books, movies, sexual promiscuity, and political atmosphere of our day have their spiritual root in the fact that men and women "did not like to retain God in *their* knowledge, [and] God gave them over to a debased mind, to do those things which are not fitting."

The very beginning of this decline can be found back in the Garden of Eden when lust tempted Adam and Eve to disobey God's Word and eat of the forbidden fruit. "So when the woman saw that the tree *was* good for food, that it *was* pleasant to the eyes, and a tree desirable to make *one* wise, she took of its fruit and ate. She also gave to her husband with her, and he ate" (Gen. 3:6). Here we see the original temptation to lust for forbidden things and to disobey God's Word.

Fortunately, God has given us His Word in Jesus Christ to save us from the destruction that disobedience brought about.

Just as disobeying God's Word produced death and destruction, so obedience to the Word of God and receiving the Word [Jesus Christ] into our lives brings eternal salvation. Additionally, in this life the exceedingly great and precious promises enable us to partake of the divine nature and escape corruption of that which is in the world through lust (2 Pet. 1:4).

The following questions will help us to explore this truth further:

How can we escape the corruption that is in the world through lust? (2 Pet. 1:4; Gal. 1:4)

In the Bible, the term "lust" applies to more than just sexual lust. What does the word "lust" mean? (1 John 2:16)

How does loving money, sex, power, fame, position, or material objects produce idolatry in our lives? (1 John 5:21)

How can properly worshiping God set us free from the corruption that is in the world through lust? (Heb. 12:1, 2)

How does worshiping sex, the creation, and other things eventually produce a debased mind? (Rom. 1:25, 28)

What is the root cause of the problems in our culture? (Rom. 1:21)

ABIDING IN THE WORD OF GOD AND OVERCOMING THE WICKED ONE

The entrance of God's Word in our lives brings light (Ps. 119:130). It purges the darkness from our inner being. It not only cleanses us but makes us righteous. In Ephesians 5:26 we read about how Jesus Christ cleanses His bride, which is the church, by "the washing of water by the word." The key to overcoming Satan is to abide in the Word of God daily. Read also 1 John 2:14.

Abiding in the Word of God enables us to overcome the wicked one. In John 8:31 we read how abiding in the Word of God produces freedom in our lives. "Then Jesus said to those Jews who believed Him, 'If you abide in My word, you are My disciples indeed. And you shall know the truth, and the truth shall set you free.'"

What kind of freedom was Jesus Christ talking about? If we go back to Romans 1:25–31, we will see the spiritual and psychological bondage that disobeying God's Word brings. Abiding in God's Word produces spiritual, psychological, and emotional freedom.

FAITH ALIVE

Based on Psalm 119:11 and Psalm 119:9, if we hide God's Word in our hearts and take heed to its counsel, then our paths will be made straight in life.

The following exercise will enable us to utilize this truth on a practical level. On the left side, we will list a temptation from the Evil One or simply a path that is wrong. On the right side we will write down a promise or commandment that will help us to overcome this temptation.

A TEMPTATION OR WRONG PATH   GOD'S WORD

1. The temptation to fear   "For God has not given us a spirit of fear, but of power and of love and of a sound mind." (2 Tim. 1:7)

2. The temptation for sexual lust   "Flee also youthful lusts: but pursue righteousness, faith, love, peace with those who call upon the Lord out of a pure heart." (2 Tim. 2:22)

3. The temptation to follow sinners in some kind of get-rich-quick scheme   "My son, if sinners entice you, do not consent." (Prov. 1:10)

Listed above are three examples of how we can avoid sin or wrong action in our lives. Using the space below, note three problem areas of your life. Then write down a verse from the Word which, hidden in your heart, can help you be an overcomer.

A TEMPTATION OR WRONG PATH   GOD'S WORD

1.

2.

3.

The Promises of God's Word Unlock Supernatural Provisions

Not only does God's Word give us the power to purify our lives, but God's Word also makes it possible for us to unlock supernatural provisions so that we can live while we are here on earth. In Matthew 6:25–34, Jesus Christ teaches that we are not to worry about the things we need to exist in this life. Our Heavenly Father will meet all of our needs through the power of His Word. In Matthew 18:18, 19, we read that Jesus Christ has given us the keys of His kingdom so that whatever we ask, He will do it for us.

Here we see the power of God's Word at work in our lives to provide us with anything we may need. The promises of the Word of God cover every situation and circumstance we could possibly face. If we read the Word of God and understand its promises for our lives, then we can boldly face the future. God has given us the keys of His kingdom to unlock supernatural provisions for our lives by the power of His Word. Our responsibility is to know what His Word says and to ask God for what we need. We can overcome in this life if we take full advantage of the supernatural provisions that He has made available to us in Christ (Phil. 4:19). We are specifically warned not to act as the Gentiles who are ignorant of God's provisions and spend all their time worrying and scheming about how to get ahead in life.

God is intimately concerned with every aspect of our lives. His Word covers provisions for not only our spiritual well-being, but our health, finances, marriage, career, sex life, and so on. Many in religious circles have had a tendency to overspiritualize the meaning of the word "salvation" and divorce it from the practical issues of life. But this is not what the Bible teaches. God, as a good heavenly Father, is not only concerned with our eternal salvation, but He is also concerned about our total well-being here on earth. The Bible does not teach a "pie in the sky" religion as the critics of Christianity have suggested.

WORD WEALTH

Salvation, *soteria.* Compare "soteriology." Deliverance, preservation, soundness, prosperity, happiness, rescue, general well-being. The word is used in both a material, temporal sense and in a spiritual, eternal sense. The New Testament especially uses the word for spiritual well-being. Salvation is a present possession (Luke 1:77; 2 Cor. 1:6; 7:10) with a fuller realization in the future (Rom. 13:11; 1 Thess. 5:8, 9).[2]

Clearly, salvation covers life in the here and now, as well as life in the hereafter. Understanding and appropriating the promises of God's Word by faith help us to overcome and live victoriously here on earth.

Listed below are some key areas in which we need supernatural provision. In the left-hand column is listed the need. In the right-hand column is listed the promise of God that will supply that need. Sometimes practical steps of obedience are necessary in order to release God's provisions.

THE NEED	THE PROMISE OF GOD'S WORD
1. Finances	"'Bring all the tithes into the storehouse, that there might be food in My house, and try Me now in this,' says the LORD of hosts, 'If I will not open for you the windows of heaven and pour out for you such a blessing that *there will* not *be room* enough *to receive it.*'" (Malachi 3:10)
	Here we see that the believer must take practical steps of obedience in order to unlock God's supernatural provision. In this area, it is not enough simply to ask. Obedience, in the area of tithes, is required.
2. Physical health	"Is anyone among you sick? Let him call for the elders of the church, and let them pray

over him, anointing him with oil in the name of the Lord. And the prayer of faith will save the sick, and the Lord will raise him up. And if he has committed sins, he will be forgiven." (James 5:14, 15)

3. Spiritual power   "But you shall receive power when the Holy Spirit has come upon you; and you shall be witnesses to Me in Jerusalem, and in all Judea and Samaria, and to the end of the earth." (Acts 1:8)

1. *Spirit-Filled Life Bible* (Nashville, TN: Thomas Nelson Publishers, 1991), 1855, "Word Wealth: 2:22 lusts."

2. Ibid., 1553, 1554, "Word Wealth: 19:9 salvation."

Lesson 12/Overcoming Satan

The enemy of God is our enemy. He never has a nice day—a day when he says, "I think I'll let up on them today." We are in a fight with a bully who has declared war on God and on us.

Why doesn't God just wipe him out? Two thoughts come to mind:

1. There are plenty of prisoners of war still to be rescued. The Lord is "not willing that any should perish, but that all should come to repentance" (2 Pet. 3:9).
2. Therefore, there is a job to do—a Great Commission (Matt. 23:18–20) and a war to be waged—a victory to be won. Indeed, victory is assured.

Our Senior Partner in both the task and the battle has already secured our triumph. His victory is our victory.

SPIRITUAL WARFARE, THE BLOOD, AND THE SPIRIT

In Revelation 12:11 we are told that we overcome Satan by the blood of the Lamb and the word of our testimony. This verse of scripture outlines the fact that we are in a great cosmic struggle with "him" (Satan), in which we are victorious and overcome by the "word of [our] testimony" and "the blood of the Lamb."

Read Revelation 12:7–10 for a glimpse of the most intense war the world has ever known, the great struggle for the hearts and souls of humankind in the invisible realm. In these verses, we see that there is a great war in the invisible realm between Michael with the angels of God and the dragon (Satan), with the fallen angels. Although this war is taking place in an unseen dimension or spiritual world, it directly affects our present reality here on earth. Earthly governments, war, peace, revival, evangelism, and other physical realities are rooted in the activity in the invisible realm. This activity is the product of intense spiritual warfare, which is not only conducted by angelic forces, but which is also waged here on the earth by believers who enter into militant intercessory prayer. This is what Dr. Peter Wagner of Fuller Theological Seminary has termed "Warfare Prayer."

In Revelation 12:7–10 we are given an overview of the battle going on in the invisible realm. With that truth in mind, how are many of the present moral, economic, political, and social conflicts of our day the result of this battle between heaven and hell at the unseen dimension?

How are pornography, drugs, the occult, violence, persecution, destruction, and the like, spawned from forces in the invisible realm? (Rev. 12:9)

How can healing, restoration, revival, evangelism, moral purity, holiness, and goodness be released by God's people through praise, worship, and spiritual warfare in the invisible realm? (Matt. 6:10)

Jesus Christ gave us powerful keys to the kingdom when He said in Matthew 16:19, "And I will give you the keys of the kingdom of heaven, and whatever you bind on earth will be bound in heaven, and whatever you loose on earth will be loosed in heaven."

Based on your understanding of Matthew 16:19, explain how we can use this power of binding and loosing in spiritual warfare.

We have been given the power of binding and loosing in spiritual warfare. Jesus Christ has given us spiritual authority to open and close doors of possibility in the invisible realm. Clearly, a great outpouring of the Holy Spirit and revival are not the products of chance or some mysterious time when God chooses to dispense blessing. These blessings are released from heaven when God's people use the keys of the kingdom to unlock heaven's supernatural provisions for an hour such as this. Revival is the surging of God's Spirit from the inner wells of the human personality. The human personality has been cleansed from sin by the blood and has been released through faith, prayer, praise, and worship to a King who died so that His power could be released fully in the midst of a dark age.

The words "they overcame him by the blood of the Lamb" refer to the fact that the blood of Jesus Christ cleanses His church from the corrupting and contaminating power of sin. When this blood of the Lamb is appropriated by the people of God, a deep cleansing and purging of the death force is activated. The blood of Jesus Christ releases the blockage inside of us so that Jesus' words in John 7:38 can be fulfilled: "He who believes in Me, as the Scripture has said, out of his heart will flow rivers of living water."

There are many reasons why the power of the blood is vital. In Revelation 12:11, we find one of the primary reasons: the blood makes it possible for a divine release of the rivers of living water to flow unhindered from our inmost being. The surging stream of God's Spirit flowing from inside of us drowns the flames of hell's fury in our lives and makes it possible for us to overcome him (the Devil) at every point.

It is the blood of Jesus Christ that makes possible the divine provision in Acts 1:8: "But you shall receive power when the Holy Spirit has come upon you; and you shall be witnesses to Me in Jerusalem, and in all Judea and Samaria, and to the end of the earth." The blood of Jesus Christ purifies us and redeems us so that God can pour out His Holy Spirit upon us.

This relationship between the blood of the Lamb and the release of the Spirit of God is a prime force in enabling us to overcome the power of the Devil. The following questions will help us apply this truth in our own lives.

How does the blood of the Lamb prepare us for a fresh outpouring of the Holy Spirit?

How does the blood of the Lamb enable us to overcome the Devil? (Rev. 12:11)

How does the power of God manifest itself in our lives through the blood of the Lamb and the outpouring of the Holy Spirit?

How does the blood of the Lamb directly release any blockages that would hinder the flow of the rivers of living water in our lives? (John 7:38)

List specific blockages that can prevent the flow of God's Spirit in your life and what the blood can do about them? (Heb. 9:14)

How can revival be released through the blood of the Lamb?

THE WORD OF GOD DIPPED IN BLOOD

In Revelation 19:13–15, we see how the Word of God is central to the end-time conflict and the present warfare here in the invisible realm. The Word of God is referred to as a sharp sword in Ephesians 6:17, where the apostle Paul says, "And take the helmet of salvation, and the sword of the Spirit, which is the word of God"; or Hebrews 4:12, "For the word of God is living and powerful, and sharper than any two-edged sword." God's Word is a powerful weapon of righteousness that not only can destroy God's enemies but circumcise the heart of believers. Revelation 19:13–15 reveals the key role that the Word of God plays in spiritual warfare.

Here we see how the blood of the Lamb and the Word of God relate directly to each other in the final conflict of human history. The Word of God, who is Jesus Christ, is clothed in a robe dipped in blood (Rev. 19:13). This is the atoning blood of Jesus Christ that was poured out for the sins of the world. In verse 14, we are told that the armies of heaven are "clothed in fine linen white and clean." This is because they have been redeemed by the blood of the Lamb. It is the blood of Jesus Christ that cleanses the church.

At the same time, it is the Word of God that acts as a sharp sword that will exercise judgment upon the nations of the earth.

When we overcome Satan by the blood of the Lamb and the word of our testimony, we are speaking the word of God and declaring that Jesus Christ has been raised from the dead. We are speaking truth and light into a dark world. We overcome Satan when we give the word of our testimony, because our testimony declares the fact that we have been born again through the Word of God and have accepted Jesus Christ by faith into our lives. This acknowledgment of the lordship of Jesus Christ in our lives destroys the power that Satan had over us. See Romans 10:8–10.

In addition, the word of our testimony declares that there is a God who really exists and rose from the dead in real space-time history. This word of our testimony, coupled with the fact that our lives have been genuinely transformed by the power of the Holy Spirit, declares to a society that denies the reality of God's existence an irrefutable proof that God is alive. The reality of our testimony is that Jesus Christ is God. The evidence of our transformed life literally destroys the Devil's lie that God does not exist or that, if He exists at all, He is some kind of New Age form of consciousness. Our testimony is living proof of the truth and reality of Christ's message. In 1 John 4:1, 2, His truth is revealed.

It is the Holy Spirit inside of us that enables us to give the word of our testimony—the confession that Jesus Christ has risen from the dead and is God. This is the Spirit of truth that lives inside of us and not the spirit of error that exists in the world. The following questions will help us understand the fact that we overcome Satan by the word of our testimony:

How does the word of our testimony affect this present world system? (John 3:33)

What happens when we give the word of our testimony and confess for the first time that Jesus Christ has been resurrected from the dead and is Lord? (Rom. 10:9, 10)

How does the power of the word of our testimony specifically overcome Satan? (Rev. 12:11)

Why is the Word of God clothed in a robe dipped in blood? (Rev. 19:13)

THE WEAPON OF THE BLOOD

From chapter 8 we learned that Satan is the accuser of the brethren (Rev. 12:10). As we have stated in an earlier chapter, there is a satanic strategy at work in attempting to destroy the word of our testimony and make us ineffective for Christ. Yet we are told that we can overcome Satan by the blood of the Lamb and the word of our testimony (Rev. 12:11).

Here we learn that the blood of the Lamb is a powerful weapon in defeating Satan. Although Satan *can* accuse us, his accusations have no legal weight, because our righteousness is based in our being washed clean in the blood of the Lamb. Every time we make a mistake or sin, God erases that sin from the page of history when we confess our sin and are washed in the blood of the Lamb.

John 1:29 says that the Lamb of God (Jesus) "takes away the sin of the world." Explain in your own words how this is so.

What practical application does that truth have in your own life as you give your testimony about Jesus Christ?

The great irony here is that it is Satan who tempts us to sin in the first place. Satan is the father of li ‚ and a master trickster. He is the driving force behind all t⊦ ⌐ckedness in this world because this present world system ﹐his doing. Thus‚ pornography in literature, music, mov⁼ ⌐nd art; greed in the marketplace; occult religions; and the power behind the drug lords are among the evils fueled by the god of this age who is Satan. It is the Christian who is swimming upstream by the power of the Holy Spirit against the philosophical flow of this world system. Yet if a Christian sins in thought, word, or deed, it is Satan—this totally impure and corrupt being and the father of this present sinful system—who dares to condemn the Christian and accuse him or her! However, the blood of Jesus Christ destroys the power of those accusations, because we are clean through the blood of Jesus Christ. In reality, our sins are not any of Satan's business because we are no longer his, but God's. We have been redeemed by the power of the blood.

 WORD WEALTH

Satan, *satan.* An opponent, or the Opponent; the hater; the accuser; adversary, enemy; one who resists, obstructs, and hinders whatever is good. *Satan* comes from the verb which means "to be an opponent," or "to withstand." As a noun, *satan* can describe any "opponent" (2 Sam. 19:21, 22). However, when the form *ha-satan* (the Adversary) occurs, the translation is usually "Satan," not his name, but his accurate description: hateful enemy. Since Satan is the Hater, he is all the more opposed to God, who is love (see 1 John 3:10–15; 4:7, 8). Mankind did not witness Satan's beginning, but by God's design shall see his end, one of ceaseless torment and humiliation (see Is. 14:12–20; Ezek. 28:16–19; Rev. 20:10).[1]

FAITH ALIVE

On a personal level, Satan attacks us as individual believers. As his name suggests, he is an opponent, accuser, adversary, enemy, one who resists, obstructs, and hinders. It is important to understand that when people come into our lives who accuse, oppose, act as an adversary, resist, obstruct, hinder or, in general, play the role of an enemy, they are often motivated by Satan. In most cases, individuals being used by Satan are completely unaware of it. They think they are "just kidding" or saying something for "your own good" or even "being led of the Lord." An individual or group, either Christian or non-Christian, can play this role. It makes no difference. The test of whether the accusation or words are from God is that, when God convicts you of sin, it is for the purpose of building you up. When Satan, through other people, condemns you, it leaves you feeling worthless, demoralized, and destroyed at some level. Please be aware. Satan will often come to us through people who are saying something in "love." But if it is love, it will strengthen us and build us up. All of us need to be accountable to brothers and sisters in Christ. Each of us needs constructive criticism in order to grow. God will use people in our lives (pastoral authority, elders, and mature members in the body of Christ) to shape and mold us. However, anyone who opposes, hates, obstructs, hinders whatever is good or acts as an adversary or enemy is not from God. We need discernment to know when God is correcting us and when Satan is attacking us.

Think about a criticism, remark, or accusation made against you; and test to see whether it is from God or an attack of Satan by answering the following questions:

Did these words that were said to me come from a healthy, strong, and positive relationship? Is this person someone I trust?

Were the words of correction spoken out of love or out of anger?

Were the words intended to improve me and build me up?

Did the person speaking those words really love me and have God's direction?

Had I violated a specific biblical principle? Was the Lord using this person to correct me?

It is possible to test any words spoken to us or written about us (in the case of those in public ministry, words may be written or published about us) by following the biblical test. Do those words do the following things?

Do the words accuse us?

Do the words attempt to hinder what is good?

Are the words spoken from hate?

Do the words attempt to obstruct us from doing what God has called us to do?

Are the words spoken in false accusation about our motives or purposes?

Do the words oppose us as people or our ministries?

If the words spoken or written about us are framed out of the above questions, then those words are energized by the powers of darkness. In other words, if the words spoken about us match up with character of Satan, then it is extremely likely that Satan may be using someone to attack us. In most cases, the individual or group that is attacking us is completely unaware that they are being used by the Adversary. Their criticism about us may come from the merely human places of believing what they are doing is "right" and may have the deeper originations of jealousy, envy, or hatred.

In our time many fruitful and legitimate ministries, ministers, and Christians have been attacked and accused unjustly because of their theology or the types of ministry that they have. Clearly there are biblical grounds for admonishment and correction. However, a lot of the criticism comes from the place of petty theological disputes that are not justified. The Lord's work is being attacked with a smallness of spirit and with pharisaical attitudes.

On the other hand, there are individual Christians, ministers, and ministries that are out of line biblically or morally. Perhaps their doctrine or teaching needs to be corrected. A case in point would have been the shepherding movement that sprang up within charismatic circles and misused the biblical principle of accountability. In recent years, there have been ministries, ministers, and individual Christians who have strayed beyond what the Bible teaches or who have been in need of correction or merely an adjustment. What is needed to avoid confusion (for Satan is the author of confusion) is wisdom, maturity, and real discernment. Since Satan is the accuser of the brethren, we can prevent his attacks by exercising discernment. Jesus advised His listeners: "Do not judge according to appearance, but judge with righteous judgment" (John 7:24).

DECLARING THE FINAL VICTORY—THE WORD OF OUR TESTIMONY

The word of our testimony is that Jesus Christ is Lord and that He has defeated sin, death, and the powers of darkness on the Cross. Jesus Christ has been resurrected from the dead. This is a powerful testimony because it literally shatters the darkness of this present satanic age and proclaims the light of the glory of the gospel of Jesus Christ. The supposed intellectual arguments of those embracing a humanistic world view come to nothing in light of Christ's resurrection from the dead. The historic proof of the resurrection of Jesus Christ echoes like a great sonic boom across the corridors of history, declaring the truth throughout the ages that Jesus Christ is Lord! Humanism becomes a mute point in light of the Resurrection. The teachings of men, such as Buddha and Muhammad, pale in comparison to the teachings of Jesus Christ, who proved His divinity by conquering death and rising from the dead. In fact, the actual resurrection of Jesus Christ from the dead makes Him completely unique among all men in history. The word of our testimony is that Jesus is Lord and He is alive, having been resurrected from the grave. The power of this truth has enabled Christians to stand before dictators and angry mobs, even to death.

Roy Hicks (international Bible teacher and author) writes, concerning Revelation 12:11:

> There is no greater biblical declaration of faith's confession. Those facing the cataclysmic travail of the last days endure it with a constant statement of the overcoming power of the blood of the Lamb and of the word of their transforming faith in Christ. Some of those declaring Christ's ultimate victory with their own lips face the fury of Satan's most vicious and personal attacks against them. Yet, their faith is unwavering, the result of an abiding relationship with Jesus Christ. This is the heart of faith's confession, based in God's Word and the blood of the Lamb, whose victory has provided the eternal conquest of Satan.[2]

In our day, the Western world has largely become what is termed a "post-Christian culture." Both humanism and New Age ideologies abound. Christians who believe in moral absolutes and biblical values are going to experience intense opposition and persecution. In Revelation 12:9 we read, "So the great dragon was cast out, that serpent of old, called the Devil and Satan, who deceives the whole world; he was cast to the earth, and his angels were cast out with him." The driving force behind political corruption, pornography, violence, the rise of the New Age and the occult, militant homosexual movements, the abortion industry, drugs, insane greed, and other evils is the serpent of old, or Satan, and his angels. It is in this environment that Christians will overcome him (the Devil) by the blood of the Lamb and the word of their testimony. The day in which we live will usher in an unprecedented conflict between good and evil. Yet it is for this day that God has promised us we will overcome by the blood of the Lamb and the word of our testimony. Our declaration, that Jesus Christ is Lord and that our lives have been transformed by Him, is the word of our testimony. In this day, Christians who uphold the authority of God's Word over cultural relativism and spiritual deception will be engaged in conflict.

Dr. Jack Hayford writes, "We can enter the conflict in confidence, knowing we shall triumph even though circumstances temporarily set us back. . . . Yet, at the same time, the presence of evil struggles for survival; though 'cast down,' the Serpent writhes viciously. Thus our temporal situation is often a fierce and sometimes painful struggle, seeming to issue in an indeterminate stand-off before our Enemy. But he only has 'a short time,' until finally the kingdom to come (Rev. 12:10) shall become the kingdom accomplished (Rev. 19—22). Let us do battle in faith and with faithfulness and, looking to that day of His ultimate kingdom, know the Holy Spirit is preparing us for kingdom victories today."[3]

Having examined the truth regarding the word of our testimony, how does this truth relate to the spiritual warfare you face as a Christian living in an environment that is often hostile to Christian beliefs?

How does the word of your testimony bring the unshakable reality of God's kingdom to wherever you work and live? (John 3:33)

Why can you be confident even if your testimony seems to be "ignored" or treated with ridicule by the people around you? (Is. 55:10, 11)

1. *Spirit-Filled Life Bible* (Nashville, TN: Thomas Nelson Publishers, 1991), 710, "Word Wealth: 1:6 Satan."

2. Ibid., 1978, "Kingdom Dynamics: Declaring the Ultimate Victory in Christ."

3. Ibid., 1977, 1978, "Kingdom Dynamics: New Testament: Agelong Warfare."

Lesson 13/Conclusion: The Blood of the Covenant and the Word of God

If the Bible teaches us anything, especially as it relates to the great truths of the blood of the covenant and the Word of God, it teaches us that our universe is constructed according to spiritual laws and that these laws cannot be violated. The great mistake of our century is for modern man to attempt to analyze and understand physical, mathematical, and biological laws, while at the same time ignoring the spiritual laws of the universe. Just as the universe runs according to certain physical laws here on earth, such as the law of gravity, so the unseen dimension or the invisible realm functions according to specific laws. Thus, in man's dealings with God, these laws must be complied with. We simply cannot come to God or relate to Him in whatever way we choose. God and the entire fabric and construction of the universe hinges on the proper functioning of spiritual law. Thus God says that we must come to Him only through faith in Jesus Christ, which is an expression of the blood covenant, and that we must understand that God's Word is absolute. These are not just religious or whimsical beliefs that can be discarded carelessly. We must understand that at the very center of the universe, in the throne room of God, the Lamb sits upon the throne. In other words, ultimate reality is the very sum total and origination of all things that stem from a specific Supreme Being with a distinct divine personality and is transcendent of any human personality. Yet this Supreme Being lives in total harmony with the very universe He constructed and governs it according to His laws.

Therefore, when we glimpse into the Book of Revelation written by the apostle John on the Isle of Patmos, we are allowed to peer into heaven where we see the most awesome vision ever imaginable—a reality that is more real than the world we live in at this present moment (read Rev. 4:8–11). At the very center of the universe is the Lamb who sits upon the throne. The automatic response of the creation, when it is in right relationship with God and not deceived by the power of sin, is to worship the Lamb. Man was created to worship God. Many elements in our culture, such as sex, materialism, and power, have become idols in false worship.

 WORD WEALTH

Worship, *proskuneo.* From *pros*, "toward," and *kuneo*, "to kiss." To prostrate oneself, bow down, do obeisance, show reverence, do homage, worship, adore. In the New Testament, the word especially denotes homage rendered to God and the ascended Christ. All believers have a one-dimensional worship, to the only Lord and Savior. We do not worship angels, saints, shrines, relics, or religious personages.[1]

In Revelation 4:11 the words, "For You created all things, and by Your will they exist and were created," describe the source of the created universe and our present reality. The Big Bang Theory, evolution, and other so-called scientific theories fail to understand that it is God and God alone who is the root source of all creation. In addition, the God who is there is not some abstract energy force or higher consciousness. He is the Lamb upon the throne!

Continuing with verses 8–13 in Revelation 5, we see that there is a reality that is far greater then the popular consensus of our day. The predominant culture today totally denies the fact of God's existence. This is evident in our news media, films, television programs, books, art, literature, and school systems. Yet this truth of God's existence is apart from and not subject to the popular opinion. Not only does the spiritual realm exist, but it exists according to what the Bible says about it. In the center of the universe is the Lamb of God. He sits upon an actual place of ultimate authority, or throne.

What does Revelation 5:8–13 teach us about the ultimate nature of the universe?

When we read Revelation 5:8–13, we see two key facts that pertain to how we overcome Satan. What are they? (Rev. 5:9, 13)

How does the fact that Jesus Christ is the Lamb who sits upon the throne affect our ability to overcome Satan? (Rev. 5:13)

How does the fact that Jesus Christ redeemed us by His blood affect our ability to overcome Satan? (Rev. 5:9)

What can we offer to Jesus, the Lamb of God, now? (Rev. 5:12)

For a time, God has permitted humankind to rebel and erect a world system that is alien to His kingdom. However, this time period is drawing to a close as the end of history approaches. The sin that deceives humankind has been destroyed by the Lamb who has redeemed us by His blood. In fact, at the very center of the universe is the final reality of the Lamb who exists, redeeming humankind by the blood. This is the very center of the universe and the very heartbeat of God reaching out in sacrificial love to men and women. What a marvelous truth that is! When we look up at the starry night sky and see the myriad display of lights twinkling in an infinite expanse, our hearts should rejoice because the universe is not empty, contrary to what the existentialists say. Nor is it a jungle where only the fittest survive. At the very center of the universe is a God of love, the Lamb upon the throne, who died so that you and I could have eternal life. Is it any wonder that part and parcel of this reality is a mighty song, a new song that gloriously proclaims the fact the Lamb was slain for the sins of the world? He purchased eternal life for each of us by His blood. What other response can there be than a mighty, eternal anthem of praise and worship that fills the darkness of the night with the splendor of His eternal glory!

WORD WEALTH

Lamb, *arnion.* Originally, a little lamb, but the diminutive force is largely missing in the New Testament. In John 21:15, *arnion* is used of young believers, while twenty-nine times in Revelation it is the title of the exalted Christ. *Arnion* is in distinct contrast to the beast. The beast is savage, cruel, hostile, and destructive. By contradistinction, our Lord as a lamb is gentle, compassionate, loving, and kind, innocently suffering and dying to atone for our sins. In the Book of Revelation, we see the lion and lamb combine the two elements of majesty and meekness.[2]

The Lamb upon the throne room of the universe is in total contrast to the god of this age or the beast. This present world system is a "dog eat dog" culture built on greed, power, and vice. God will bring this satanic system down, and the Lamb will rule upon the earth. As believers in Jesus Christ, our responsibility is to partner with the Lamb and to overcome Satan with the word of our testimony and the blood of the Lamb.

After understanding the truth of our partnering with Jesus Christ, what is our personal responsibility, together with Jesus Christ, to overcome Satan with the word of our testimony and the blood of the Lamb? (Rev. 12:11)

How does the fact that we are partnering with the One who sits upon the very throne of the universe affect our perspective as we face life's battles? (Eph. 2:6)

How should this reality of our partnering with the real God who rules in glory upon the throne of the universe change the way we view every single circumstance and the seemingly "ordinary" events in our lives? In fact, when we are in relationship with Him, are there such things as merely "ordinary" events?

The blood of the covenant and the authority of God's Word are two powerful keys in securing our victory over the powers of darkness. The power of the beast has been destroyed by the power of the blood of the Lamb and the authority of His Word. The Beast prevails over the present system of lies and governs many on our planet. The time is coming quickly when this truth of God's victory over Satan will be manifest upon this planet. Our responsibility, in this time of transition, is literally to over-come him (Satan) with the word of our testimony and the blood of the Lamb. As we saw in Revelation, the Lamb upon the throne is being worshiped by the saints, the angels, the living creatures, and the elders (Rev. 5:8–14). As the saints worship God and sing a new song, they are infused with the life of God Himself. Man becomes like what he worships. If a man worships money, sex, power and vanity, then he becomes a corrupt being, as empty as the object he worships. If men and women worship God, they become like the Lamb upon the throne and are filled with His presence.

In Revelation 21:9–11 a great mystery is revealed. The mys-tery is that, in some supernatural capacity, we are the building blocks of a brand new world or heavenly city in which Jesus Christ is the chief cornerstone. In Revelation 21:2, we are given a further description. "Then I, John, saw the holy city, New Jerusalem, coming down out of heaven from God, prepared as a bride adorned for her husband." In Scripture Christians are described as the bride of Christ. Ephesians 5:25–27 states that Christ gave Himself for the church, "that He might present her to Himself a glorious church, not having spot or wrinkle or any such thing, but that she should be holy and without blemish." Two things are at work here. First, we are described as the bride of Christ. Second, the holy city, New Jerusalem, is "prepared as a bride adorned for her husband." In some capacity, the New Jerusalem will be a living city in which every believer will be part of a structure as living components.

What is the purpose of our being redeemed by the blood of the Lamb? We are to enter into an intimate relationship with the God of all the universe. Obviously, earthly words, such as "bride" and "city" cannot fully describe a relationship that is beyond human understanding. The Scripture uses the phrase "prepared as a bride" when describing the city of New Jerusalem. Clearly, we are not going to become bricks and mortar. We are going to, in some supernatural sense, become living stones in a spiritual house or city. In 1 Peter 2:4, 5, this concept of a living stone is described:

Coming to Him *as to* a living stone, rejected indeed by men, but chosen by God *and* precious, you also, as living stones, are being built up a spiritual house, a holy priesthood, to offer up spiritual sacrifices acceptable to God through Jesus Christ.

We are to be *living stones* in the supernatural structure of the New Jerusalem. Unlike any earthly city, the light of the New Jerusalem will be the glory of the Lamb and the light of God. In Revelation 21:22, 23, we read: "But I saw no temple in it, for the Lord God Almighty and the Lamb are its temple. The city had no need of the sun or the moon to shine in it, for the glory of God illuminated it. The Lamb *is* its light."

We are reading about a world that is so far beyond this present earthly existence that it is difficult for our finite minds to comprehend. In Ephesians 2:19–22 the apostle Paul writes:

Now, therefore, you are no longer strangers and foreigners, but fellow citizens with the saints and members of the household of God, having been built on the foundation of the apostles and prophets, Jesus Christ Himself being the chief corner*stone*, in whom the whole building, being fitted together, grows into a holy temple in the Lord, in whom you are also being built together for a dwelling place of God in the Spirit.

This is the purpose of redemption by the blood of the Lamb. That is why it says in Ephesians 1:7, "In Him we have redemption through His blood, the forgiveness of sins, according to the riches of His grace." "But now in Christ Jesus you who were once far off have been brought near by the blood of Christ" (Eph. 2:13). It is the blood of Jesus Christ that redeems us and makes us part of the temple of the living God. The temple of God and the New Jerusalem are living, and we are part of it in Christ.

The truths that we are the bride of Christ and living stones in God's temple reflect a supernatural mystery. The following questions will help us apply those truths in our lives:

What does the Bible mean by calling us "the bride of Christ"? (Eph. 5:25–27)

What does the Bible mean when it says we are living stones in God's temple? (1 Pet. 2:4, 5)

How does the fact that the Bible calls me the bride of Christ affect my life right now? (Rev. 22:17)

How does the fact that the Bible calls me a living stone in God's temple affect the way I live my life here on earth? (1 Pet. 2:5)

In Revelation 21:27 we read about who will be allowed to enter the heavenly city. "But there shall by no means enter it anything that defiles, or causes abomination or a lie, but only those who are written in the Lamb's Book of Life." It is the blood of

Jesus Christ and our acceptance of the blood-covenant sacrifice of Jesus Christ that cleanses us from all sin and allows us to enter the heavenly city.

When the Bible says, "They overcame him [Satan] by the blood of the Lamb and the word of their testimony," it means that our destiny is secured by Christ. We have a fantastic future and great destiny as part of the living temple of God. Our God is the Creator, and He doesn't intend for us to be dull bricks in some stuffy, old temple, as religious tradition so often suggests. We are going to be part of the most fantastic journey ever imagined. It is because of the blood of Jesus Christ.

Inherent in a great spiritual battle between God and Satan is the reality that Satan has gone to great lengths to blind people to the glorious reality of our destiny in Christ. One of his prime strategies is to make our eternal destiny with Christ seem dull and boring while making sin look alluring. Sin is only alluring to those who have not yet glimpsed the heavenly vision. There is a future so bold, alive, creative, and dynamic that it completely transcends the human imagination.

The blood of the covenant and obeying the Word of God will gain us entrance into this paradise. Remember, back in the Garden of Eden Adam and Eve chose to reject God's Word as the final authority in their lives. They fell from grace and triggered the death force of sin to be injected into creation and the human race. However, God provided a way home. The way home is only through the blood of the covenant and obeying the Word of God. The way out of Paradise was disobeying the Word of God. The way back into God's presence is through the blood of Christ and by receiving that Word of God. The Word regenerates us and becomes flesh in us as we live in Him. When Adam and Eve rejected the Word of God, the spring of the life force was expelled from our planet. However, when we receive the Word into our hearts by faith in Christ, the springs of eternal life begin to be activated.

The following questions will help us to understand how the Word of God and the blood of the covenant enable us to overcome:

How did disobeying the Word of God cause the Fall of Man? (Rom. 5:17–19)

How does obeying the Word of God bring us back to God? (Heb. 11:6)

How does obedience to the Word of God and obeying the terms of the blood covenant give us access to heaven and eternal life? (John 5:24)

In Revelation 22:1–3 we read about the return to Paradise.

And He showed me a pure river of water of life, clear as crystal, proceeding from the throne of God and of the Lamb. In the middle of the street, and on either side of the river, *was* the tree of life, which bore twelve fruits, each *tree* yielding its fruit every month. The leaves of the tree *were* for the healing of the nations. And there shall be no more curse, but the throne of God and of the Lamb shall be in it, and His servants shall serve Him.

In Genesis 2 we read about the tree of life and the tree of the knowledge of good and evil. Adam and Eve disobeyed God's Word and rejected it as the final authority in their lives. The result was the fall of humankind and the tragedy of human history that has played out through the centuries. Yet God loved us so much that He provided a way back. The descendants of Adam and Eve have a choice, and they can choose to accept the Word that Adam and Eve rejected. The Word of God is Jesus Christ. When we receive Him into our lives, we receive God's Word into our lives. Jesus Christ was in the Garden of Eden with Adam and Eve, because Jesus Christ is the Word of God.

But it was only through the blood covenant and the blood of Jesus Christ that the Word could be received into human lives. It is the blood of the Lamb that provides the cleansing so that the Word can become active in our lives. Jesus Christ is the Lamb who was slain for the sins of the world. He is also the Word become flesh.

The release of eternal life in our lives is made possible by the blood of the Lamb and the word of our testimony. When we are cleansed by the blood of the Lamb and are regenerated by the Word of God, the flow of God's life pours through us. God is "life" itself. He is the river of life (Rev. 22:1). The finished work on the Cross, the release of Christ's sacrificial blood, and the activation of the blood of the covenant through faith in the full authority of the Word of God allow the cleansing streams of heaven's glory to be poured through our lives.

This glory is released when we worship the Lamb upon the throne and sing a new song out of our inmost being. The worship of the Lamb upon the throne releases the presence of God in our midst. The blood of Jesus Christ paves the way for the release of this glory. This is how we overcome him (Satan) by the word of our testimony and the blood of the Lamb. These two provisions make it possible for us to experience Revelation 22:1, not as just some far-off event, but as a present, moment-by-moment, experiential reality. The power of Satan is mortally crushed when the floodgates of God's river of glory are released in the lives of believers. The serpent of old, who deceived the human race in the Garden of Eden and who wages war against the saints, cannot withstand the fountains of glory that are released through praise and worship to the Lamb upon the throne!

1. *Spirit-Filled Life Bible* (Nashville, TN: Thomas Nelson Publishers, 1991), 1967, "Word Wealth: 4:10 worship."

2. Ibid., 1969, "Word Wealth: 6:1 Lamb."